May 18, 2020

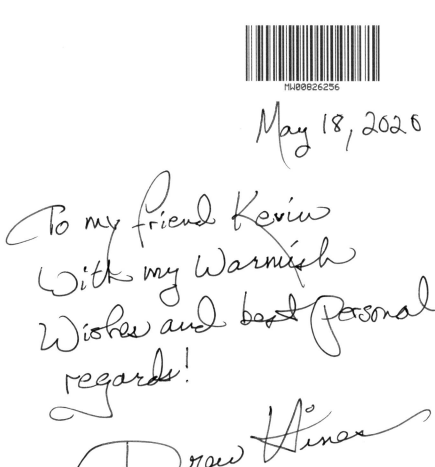

To my friend Kevin
With my Warmish
Wishes and ~~best~~ Personal
regards!

Drew Hiner
Philippians 4:19

In Mountain Shadows

The story of
WASHINGTON BAPTIST CHURCH
Greer, SC • 1819 - 2019

Drew Hines

In Mountain Shadows

by Drew Hines

ISBN: 978-1-940645-71-1

Greenville, South Carolina
PRINTED IN THE UNITED STATES OF AMERICA

NOTICE:

Thank you to those who donated photos for our history book. However, due to age and low resolution, some photos may not appear clear. Please note that every effort was taken to assure names and content were accurate to the best of our ability from information given.

In Mountain
Shadows

In mountain shadows my faith is built
As through the valleys I pass.
In the shelter of the towering hills
I find a strength that lasts.

Drew Hines

TABLE OF CONTENTS

FOREWORD

It seems virtually impossible to condense 200 years of a church's history into one book, but this volume represents my effort to do just that. It would also seem impractical to think that one person could do it alone. Indeed, *In Mountain Shadows* has been a team effort from start to finish, and it has been a labor of love for all involved.

Oddly enough, there have been just two previous attempts to chronicle the history of Washington Baptist Church over the past two centuries. In May, 1901, at the request of the church, Mr. J.T. Henerey, a deacon and much-respected church leader, wrote a brief, five-page essay highlighting the history of the church up to that point. While sketchy at best, it still gives us a good snapshot of how, where and why Washington was organized. It remained the standard history of our church for well over a century.

And then Mrs. Vivian Langford entered the picture. No one has loved the history and heritage of Washington Baptist Church more than Vivian. She had a vision to open a history room in our church. That one room became two, and now one can literally spend hours there poring over pictures, newspaper clippings, and historical documents relating to our church's long and rich history. These materials are very well organized and ready for study. These rooms has been invaluable for my own research for this book. In 2014, Mrs. Langford published, at her own expense, *A Stroll Through the History of the First 195 Years of Washington Baptist Church, Greer, SC.* Those fortunate enough to have obtained a copy of this book have been blessed and well informed. That volume, along with another she compiled featuring pictures and biographical sketches of previous pastors, have been a tremendous assistance to me. So a huge word of thanks and gratitude goes out to Mrs. Vivian Langford for her tireless efforts in reminding us of the importance of studying our past. And I would certainly be remiss if I didn't mention the role her husband, Jim, has played in all this. His encouragement and assistance, I know, have meant so much to Vivian and to us! Thank you, Mr. and Mrs. Langford!

Also, a very special word of thanks goes out to our 200th anniversary committee, which has been chaired so capably by Ms. Wanda Moore, and is composed of a group of faithful and dedicated members who have seen this celebration through from start to finish. They include:

Patsy Edney	Elaine Parris
Elaine Green	Candace Rathbone
Ronnie Knight	Karla Ross
Wanda Moore, Chair	John Susie
Bonnie Mussman	Wanda Vaughn

Their tireless efforts have insured that this momentous and monumental event is celebrated in appropriate fashion. They have also assisted me in the preparation of this book in significant ways. Thank you again for your hard work!

Mrs. Candace Rathbone has used her considerable talents, not only in the design of this book, but also in the artwork and logos used in other areas of this year-long celebration. This book simply would not have been possible without her.

Dr. Anne Blythe, historian, novelist and friend, met with our committee and offered great assistance and wise counsel. I also call to mind my dear friend and mentor, the late Mann Batson, who was a teacher and encourager to me for several years. I regret that Mr. Batson died before he was able to see this book. Through the years that I had the joy of knowing him, he encouraged me and occasionally prodded me to sit down and write. And though he received his "upward call" on May 5, 2017, I would suspect that he would be glad one of his protégé finally took up the pen and wrote! You will find that I cite several of his books in this one.

To the staff of Washington Baptist Church — Rev. Joe Price, Ms. Karla Ross, Mr. Travis Henson, Mrs. Toni Arms, Mrs. Dana Salsman, Mrs. Allison Grubbs, and Mrs. Sherry Smith — I wish to say "thanks" for the times you not only encouraged me and assisted me, but also for the times you covered for me during this project. We are truly blessed as a church to have these loyal and faithful servants. I also call to mind the important role the deacons of Washington have played in all of this. They allowed me the time to get away for a couple of weeks to work on this book. And they have, throughout this process, offered many warm words of encouragement and much-needed prayers.

To my late parents, Charles J. and June Elliott Hines, I wish to express my deepest love and appreciation for instilling within me at a very early age a love for reading and learning, in general, and history in particular. Being surrounded by books on history as well as our frequent trips and tours of historic sites inspired me early on to love the past.

To my wonderful wife, Suzanne, our children Miranda and Andrew, their spouses Chris and Megan, and our four beautiful grandchildren, June, Bennett, Cece, and Landree, I wish to express my deepest love and appreciation. Their support and encouragement have inspired me in so many ways. I cannot imagine my years as a minister of the Gospel without Suzanne by my side.

And, of course, to my beloved church family at Washington Baptist Church, thank you for allowing me the pleasure, honor and privilege of being your pastor for over eighteen years now! This has been a joyous journey every step of the way. I dedicate this book to you — to your past, your present, and your bright, promising future. I celebrate those saints who have stood for, prayed for, supported and led our church. And to those who now, and will in the future, take up the cause of Christ here at Washington: To you, I commend this history. Read it and learn from it.

And finally, and most importantly, I dedicate this volume to our Lord and Savior Jesus Christ! This is really His story, because this is His church He established and for which He died.

Soli deo gloria!

May God richly bless His church in the years ahead!

Drew Hines, DMin
October 2019
Lake Junaluska, North Carolina

In Mountain
Shadows

INTRODUCTION

Are you interested in Washington Baptist Church's long-lasting history and how our church has victoriously waved the banner of Christ these 200 years? How did we come to be? Where were we first located? Who was our first pastor? What have been the major milestones in our many enduring years of serving our Lord here at Washington? What are our precious memories? These questions and others will be answered as you begin to read in this book the journey of Washington Baptist over the past two centuries. Note: a little history perspective — James Monroe was the president of the United States in the year 1819 when Washington Baptist Church was established. He was our country's fifth president. We have had forty presidents since then.

We want you to learn about the journey taken by our church over these 200 years to become the church it is today. These are some amazing and powerful stories of pastors, lay men and women who served tirelessly and boldly in our earlier years to establish the foundation of faith on which this church has continued in His service. We have progressed from a small gathering of committed and hopeful Christians to a church membership of almost a thousand, still proclaiming the same message of hope for all — that God, our Heavenly Father, the Almighty and Sovereign One, has given mankind the opportunity to have an eternal life with Him and His people through the sacrificial death of His Son, Jesus Christ, by trusting in Him as our Lord and Savior.

Who better to tell our story than our current pastor, Dr. Drew Hines. Dr. Hines has been pastor of Washington Baptist Church since June 2001. Let me introduce you to Drew: a pastor, preacher, soul winner, husband, father, grandfather, friend, comforter, confidant. He is a lover of God, His Word, and the souls of men and women. He's also a historian. Ask him a question about this community or the Dark Corner of northern Greenville County and the role of the churches in this region of South Carolina, and he will enlighten you with stories and tales he has gathered from his many interactions with historians and folks in this area. Some are reflected in his writing of this book.

Drew was born in Greensboro, North Carolina, in April of 1954. The second son of the late Charles J. and June Elliott Hines, Drew's family moved to South Carolina when he was in the tenth grade. Drew played high school football and was very active in student life at Wade Hampton High School in Greenville. There was a curiosity about him — especially about history. He recalls that it was his parents who instilled in him a love of the past. Among other historical travels, there were trips to Civil War battlegrounds and an early journey to Washington, D.C. that made a lasting impression on him. These early lessons fueled his passion for history.

Drew became a Christian at the age of sixteen while a member of Lee Road Baptist Church in Taylors, South Carolina. Early on, he felt the call to ministry and then yielded to the call when he was twenty-four. He is a graduate of the University of South Carolina in Columbia, and received Master of Divinity and Doctor of Ministry degrees from the Southern Baptist Theological Seminary in Louisville, Kentucky.

Drew's first pastorate was Foster Avenue Baptist Church in Louisville. He later became pastor of several churches in South Carolina including Ebenezer Welcome Baptist Church in Landrum, Pleasant Grove Baptist Church in Greer, and the First Baptist Church of Andrews. He also served as Director of Missions for the Moriah Baptist Association in Lancaster, South Carolina and as Director of Pastoral Ministries for the South Carolina Baptist Convention. Drew has been married to the former Suzanne Morris since 1976. They have two children — Miranda (Chris), Andrew (Megan) — and four grandchildren.

During Drew's eighteen-year tenure at Washington, the church has experienced considerable growth in our programs, ministries, membership and in our mission efforts both globally and locally. Our church is committed to serving our God boldly and faithfully in this twenty-first century at a time when the modern-day church is being attacked by a worldly culture of non-believers. Although we have witnessed churches across the country experiencing declining memberships — some even closing their doors — through God's blessings and our continued dependence on Him to lead us, we have stayed true to the meaning and purpose of the church, and God has blessed us accordingly. I truly believe if those pastors and leaders of yesteryear could speak, they would say, "Thanks be to God for His faithfulness through the years."

Blessed are those whose God is the Lord.

It is so important to remember and to recall those people and events that frame who we are. Throughout the Bible we are told to remember. In the Old Testament, God was often telling His people to remember Him and what He had done for His people. In the New Testament, Jesus told His disciples to "remember me." We, too, need to remember our gracious God and those individuals and events that have brought us to where we are today as a church, and Drew Hines has done just that in this book. We are celebrating in this 200th anniversary year not only our past and its many blessings, but also what God has in His plans for the future.

To God be the glory, great things He has done!

Drew's vision for writing this book is to share his love for our church and our history with all of you. He is honoring, through his book, everyone who has been a part of this church's history and each undertaking, whether big or small, which has contributed to Washington Baptist Church as it is today. Through joys and sorrows, struggles and triumphs, Washington Baptist Church has had a story to tell — a story that has not been diminished or compromised by circumstances, a story that has not been defeated. It is a story of God's amazing love for all — a story that Washington Baptist Church continues to tell.

Although we may take for granted life's precious gifts,
we are ever aware of memories that emerge out of the past.

To you Drew, our beloved pastor:

On behalf of your Washington Baptist Church family, I want to thank you for writing this book — this tremendous and laborious undertaking. Every member of Washington Baptist Church, past and present, is a piece of the fabric of this colorful tapestry that is our church. You have blessed us through the writing of this history, and you have served well those who came before you. You have often said that when you were ordained to the ministry, you were told by your ordaining pastor, Rev. Pat Perry, to preach the Word and to love God's people. That was your calling … and that is what you have done so well. This book is your gift to us, your church family and friends. Thank you for this lasting and greatly cherished tribute.

Blessings,
Wanda Moore, Chairperson
200th Anniversary Committee

"One generation will commend Your works to another
and will tell of Your mighty acts."
Psalm 145:4 (NIV)

Great is Thy faithfulness.

——┤ Chapter One ├——
ROOTS

The earliest residents of the Washington community were the Indians, mostly Cherokee, who lived along the rich bottom lands of the Tyger and Enoree rivers, and hunted in the dense upcountry forests, teeming with wildlife. According to local tradition, supported by frequent discoveries of Indian artifacts, there was a Cherokee settlement of some sort behind Washington Church where the Castle Rock subdivision is now located.

For long centuries, these people lived undisturbed by the incursion of the white man. All that changed in the mid 1700s as adventurous traders and explorers trekked into the back country in search of fortune and opportunity. They came slowly at first, establishing outposts from which they could make contact with the natives. Later they started permanent settlements. Treaties that colonial governors had earlier made with the Indians were quickly forgotten by the white man, hungry for fertile farm land. A boundary line was surveyed, running roughly from the Blockhouse on Tryon Mountain to an established point just south of Greenville. The current Greenville/Spartanburg county line follows the old Indian boundary today. White pioneers began settling on the Indian side of the boundary, inciting the wrath of the Cherokee. Bloody massacres ensued, the most notable of which was the Hampton massacre that took place just east of Greer off US Highway 29. Today, a stone marker stands just off the highway to remind passersby of the infamous event that took place in 1776.

As a result of this and other confrontations with the Indians, a line of frontier forts was built around the area. Fort Gowen, Fort Prince, Earle's Fort and Wood's Fort were erected to offer settlers protection from brutal Indian attacks.

During the American Revolution, the upper reaches of Greenville and Spartanburg counties played an important role in the effort to secure freedom. Several skirmishes took place in the area. Most fighting took place between patriotic settlers and Tories, as they were called. Tories were area residents who remained loyal to the British king. Robbers, thieves and marauders often aligned themselves to the Tory cause because the British Regulars encouraged them to murder and loot the patriots during their frequent raids. The two most notorious and infamous of the Tory raiders were "Bloody Bill" Bates and "Bloody Bill" Cunningham. Frontier patriots were constantly on guard for these attacks and fought valiantly to win the war for independence.

THE PEOPLE

Most of the settlement in the Washington community took place after the Revolution. In the late eighteenth and early nineteenth centuries, floods of Scotch-Irish people made the long, arduous journey down the "Great Wagon Road" from Pennsylvania into Virginia, and then on into the Carolinas.

The Scotch-Irish were a hardy breed of people. Originating in Scotland and the border country of Northern England, they were sturdy and tough by nature and Presbyterian by faith. Transplanted to Northern Ireland by the British monarchs, their job was to maintain British holdings in Ulster and keep the fiery Irish Catholic revolutionaries in check. A series of famines later forced massive migrations of these adventurous people to America. Their fighting spirit inspired William Penn and the Quakers of Pennsylvania to offer them lands in the western counties of their state. There, they served as buffers from Indian attack. Later, the desire for more opportunity enticed them to move further south. Some settled in Virginia. Many came to the Carolinas. Several chose to settle in the Greenville and Spartanburg districts. Elite Charlestonians of British and French descent looked down condescendingly upon the Scotch-Irish and thought them to be an inferior breed. Yet they, like the Pennsylvanians before them, were glad they were settling the upcountry, serving as a wall of protection from hostile Indian attack. Settlers of English, French and German descent also populated the area. But by far, the majority of the early settlers in the Washington community had Scotch-Irish roots.

EARLY ROADS

One of the most attractive features of the area to the early settlers was its proximity to important and well-traveled roads. One of the closest was the old Rutherford Road, which connected Rutherfordton, North Carolina to Greenville, South Carolina. Most of these old roads followed the paths of earlier Indian trails. The old Rutherford Road meandered out of the foothills of North Carolina and traveled south, passing through Landrum and Gowensville, intersecting the old Blackstock Road. It then turned near Berry's Mill and onto present day South Carolina Highway 101, then turning on to Milford Church Road, going past Milford Baptist Church. Then it turned on to present day McElhaney Road, crossed

South Carolina Highway 290, and entered Greenville near the old Southern Worsted Mill. This was an important trading route and was the road, historians tell us, that "Bloody Bill" Bates was carried along after being apprehended in Polk County, North Carolina. He was taken to the Greenville jail and was soon killed by the son of one of his victims who sought revenge for the brutal massacre of his family. This said route was followed for years. A Greenville County map from 1882 shows the Rutherford Road taking this route. Later, Highway 14 took up at Berry's Mill and came through the Washington community on its way to Greer, some five miles away. (Howard, *Dark Corner Heritage*, p. 55)

The earliest settlers of the Washington community were a tough bunch, hardened by the constant threat of Indian attack, a hard-fought Revolutionary War and the perpetual possibility of drought, disease and starvation.

Another important early road in the area was the Gap Creek Road — a toll road proceeding from the Saluda Gap in North Carolina. This was one of the most heavily traveled roads in the upcountry because it connected Buncombe County, North Carolina, and regions farther west with the trading markets of South Carolina, and, ultimately, Charleston. Mountain farmers regularly traveled this road with wagon loads of mountain cabbages, potatoes, apples and chestnuts. Herds of cattle, swine and even turkeys were herded along the Gap Creek Road. Inns and taverns sprang up along this highway to accommodate the constant, non-stop flow of traffic. The Gap Creek Road came out of the mountains, crossed what is now South Carolina Highway 11, came past the Dickey plantation in the Highland community, and then proceeded down what is now known as West Gap Creek Road, a road that still bears the old name. It took up the route of present-day Highway 14 at Washington Church and then followed East Gap Creek Road all the way to Duncan. From there it proceeded to Columbia, and finally on to Charleston (Howard, *Dark Corner Heritage*, p. 57). These roads, without a doubt, encouraged the settlement and growth of the Washington community.

EARLY FARMING AND INDUSTRY

Most of the early settlers around Washington were farmers who made their living from the rocky, clay soil of the area. Some were given large land grants for service rendered during the American Revolution. Many purchased small parcels, and with hard work they were able to survive — and even thrive. Others utilized power harnessed from swift creeks and rivers, and erected gristmills and sawmills to accommodate their neighbors' needs. Still other enterprising souls created early factories using the power of running water to manufacture yarn and cloth. Just north of Washington Baptist is the site of one of the first textile mills in the area. In 1820, native New Englander John Weaver established a yarn mill at the site of what would later be known as Berry's Mill. Weaver also operated a grist mill and a sawmill at the same location. In 1850, 100 bales of cotton were used in the production of yarn in the Weaver Mill. The factory employed three males and ten females, and by 1860 boasted the use of 500 spindles in its yarn production. John Weaver died on November 25, 1862, and was buried in the Highland Baptist Church cemetery (Batson, *Water Powered Gristmills and Their Owners*, p. 163).

Obviously, the earliest settlers of the Washington community were a tough bunch, hardened by the constant threat of Indian attack, a hard-fought Revolutionary War, and the perpetual possibility of drought, disease and starvation. Their descendants to this day carry these same traits of faith, industry and strong character. These are the roots of Washington Baptist Church.

Chapter Two
BEGINNINGS
1819-1844

The beginnings of Washington Baptist Church are veiled in mystery. Why was the church founded in the first place? What prompted them to choose the name "Washington"? Unfortunately, some of these questions may remain unanswered because many of the early records of the church, and, indeed, many of the later records of the church have been lost. And that presents its own challenges when trying to write a history book.

How do churches begin in the first place? Some begin quite intentionally, well-planned and executed. In other words, an existing church sees a need for a viable Christian witness in a particular area or community, so it sends its people and its resources to that place to plant a church. Several of the oldest churches in Greenville County, for example, helped give birth to early congregations that thrive to this very day. In old associational records, it is quite common to see a church established as "an arm" of an older congregation.

Another way churches begin is unintentionally, when disagreements among church members reach the point where the two groups believe further fellowship is no longer possible. One group will then leave the existing church and start another. It is true that sometimes Baptists multiply by division. Baptists have a democratic, congregational form of church polity that allows them to make independent decisions about the direction they take. There are no bishops, popes or presbyteries to tell them what to do. Baptists are free to leave a church in order to start another or just to "take over" the one they're in. Many good, strong Baptist churches exist today because a group of church members became disillusioned in one church and decided to start another. This is a testimony of the grace and goodness of Almighty God that He can take a hurtful and negative situation like church division and use it for the benefit of His kingdom. He truly is the God who "works all things together for good to them that love God, to them that are called according to His purpose" (Romans 8:28).

Churches can also be born out of crisis. When people are shaken to their very foundations by some catastrophe, they often, and correctly, turn their attention to their Creator, who gives them meaningful purpose in life. Church histories often tell of congregations forming in the aftermath of earthquakes, hurricanes or tornadoes.

In 1819, the year Washington Baptist Church was organized, an economic depression crippled our young nation. Cotton prices tumbled, and the entire state of South Carolina suffered as a result. (Edgar, *South Carolina, A History*, p. 330). Maybe this economic downswing and its results played a role in Washington's beginnings.

The most reasonable explanation, however, is that as the area gradually grew and more Christians moved in, a need for a church arose since there were few existing fellowships in the immediate area. In the day before there were faster forms of transportation and good roads, most people chose to work and worship in their own communities. As a result, churches began springing up in the area. Country churches, small and close-knit, were soon constituted. It could be assumed that this was the case with Washington. According to *The Bicentennial History of Brushy Creek Baptist Church of Taylors, S.C.*, which was authored by Susan Kahl, "Washington Baptist Church became an arm of Brushy Creek in 1819 and was constituted as an independent body within the same year" (p. 16). Brushy Creek began much earlier in 1794. Brushy Creek became known as the "mother" church of many local churches, including Clear Springs, Mountain Creek, Pleasant Grove, Rocky Creek, and Rock Hill.

WASHINGTON'S BIRTH

W.D. Berry

Washington's first historian, J.T. Henerey, writes in his 1901 account of the church's beginnings,

"Early in the year 1819, a little band of Baptists used to meet under the large white oaks near Brother W.D. Berry's wood shop, about one quarter of a mile from this spot."

According to Berry family information, William Berry settled early in the Washington community. He is buried in the Mosteller cemetery high on a hill across from Lakeview Steakhouse on South Carolina Highway 14. His tombstone records his age at death as 96, though family tradition says he was more like 106 or 107. Although details about William Berry are sketchy, it is known that he owned a considerable amount of land in the area. Some of that land he would later

The State of South Carolina,
Know all men by these presents, That
I Mrs. D. Berry of Greenville Cou̲████
State aforesaid, for and in consideration
nineteen dollars & fifty cents to me paid by
the Washington Baptist Church, through the
hands of Mrs. I. Bates one of the present Deacons
of said Church, Have Granted, Bargained, Sold
and Released, and by these presents do grant, bar
gain sell and release, unto the said Mr. I. Bates, tog
~~her with the other Deacons of the~~ ████████
to their Successors in Office forever a certa
piece or lot of land whereon the said Church
now Stands, being in Greenville County and
State aforesaid, Beginning at a Stone in the S.
corner of said lot and runs Thence N 51½. E. 3. 00 C.
to a Stooping P.O. Thence N 38 W 7. 30. to Stone
Thence S 50 W 5. 45 to Stone. Thence S 12 ~~────~~
Stone Thence S 79. E 5. 90 to the begin~~ning~~
Containing Three Acres & nine tenths (3⁹⁄₁₀) of a
Acre be the same more or less   Together with
all and Singular the rights members. Heredit
ments, and Appurtenances thereunto belongin

These two pages are a photo of Washington's church deed
presented by W.D. Berry.

or in anywise incident or appertaining, To have
and to hold all and singular the said premises
for the use & purpose of said Church, together

~~with all the~~ privileges of a Public Burying ground
~~and also the right of a public road of access~~
And I do hereby bind myself my Heirs. Execut?
or Admrs. to warrant and forever defend the said
premises, against me and against every other
person or persons whomsoever lawfully claim
ing the same or any part thereof,

In Witness whereof I hereunto set my hand
and Seal, this 23d day of February   in the year

Signed sealed & delivered
in the presents of
W. P. Howell
_____
The _____
This is a correct Plat
_____ Baptist
_____ Lot, Containing
Three & nine tenths Acres,
Laid down by a Scale of
5 Chains per inch,—

A portion of the church deed is also depicted on the
cover of this history book.

donate to the fledgling congregation. Quoting Henerey again:

> "Sometime during the year (1819) they erected
> a log house near the northeast corner of this
> edifice (the old sanctuary) and on October
> 30,1819 they were constituted a Gospel church."

Again, tradition holds that William Berry donated land to the church on the single condition that there would never be a cemetery on the property. Berry owned a beautiful twin spring close by, from which he got his drinking water, and he feared burials nearby would foul his water supply. William Berry's son, W.D. Berry, would later, in 1876, sell the church 3.9 acres of land for $19.50. (Langford, *A Stroll Through the History of the First 195 Years of Washington Baptist Church, Greer, S.C., 1819-2014*, p. 5).

THE WASHINGTON NAME

One of the great unanswered questions of Washington's origins is how and why did they choose the name "Washington"? Obviously, the name itself came from the father of our country, George Washington, who was, and remains to this day, one of the most admired and respected leaders in history. Maybe they named the church after him. There's another theory, too. In the earliest days, Greenville County was called the Washington District. Perhaps they named the church more after the geographical location than after the president himself. Whatever the reason, the name "Washington" has forever been immortalized by the church.

Again, from J.T. Henerey, "On October 30, 1819, they were constituted a Gospel church by a presbytery consisting of Elders Lewis Rector, Isaac Lamance and William King, assisted by deacons John Sparks, James

West, Robert Foster, and Jacob Bridwell."

As already noted, it is probable that Washington Baptist Church had a very early connection with Brushy Creek Baptist Church in Taylors, but it is also interesting that the presbytery organized to constitute Washington consisted of some men who had close ties with Reedy River Baptist Church of Travelers Rest. Isaac Lamance (sometimes spelled Lemons, Lemmons, or Lammence) pastored Reedy River from 1809 until 1819, the year of Washington's founding. And William King served as Reedy River's church clerk from 1800 to 1804, and also served as her pastor on two different occasions, 1803-1809 and 1826-1829 (Batson, *A History of Reedy River Baptist Church,* pp. 45-46). Reedy River, constituted in 1778, was instrumental in starting several area churches. Brushy Creek and Reedy River both most likely worked in partnership to begin Washington Baptist Church.

REV. ISAAC LAMANCE
(1819-1838)

Rev. Isaac Lamance was called to be Washington's first pastor in 1819. Little is known about the origin of this humble man of God, but we do know that down through the years he gained the reputation of being a devout and faithful worker for the Lord. As previously mentioned, he had served as pastor of Reedy River Baptist Church from 1803 to 1819. He evidently preached in a number of area churches and religious assemblies during his tenure at Reedy River. According to the minutes of the Reedy River Baptist Church:

> "Money was made up in 1816 to buy Brother
> Lemons a horse. Brother Lemons was a
> missionary and had to go from one arm of

the church to the other. Therefore, the church
felt it her obligation to provide
him with transportation"
(Batson, *History of the Upper Part of
Greenville County, S.C.*, p. 247).

Lamance was an able preacher and effective communicator of the Gospel. One hearer noted that "his style of preaching was said to be of an allegorical character. It didn't matter what a literal reading of the text might mean, it had a spiritual significance that must be evolved or brought out. Much time was taken up unfolding the spiritual mysteries embodied in the text of his choice. He was uneducated, but spoke with considerable fluency, great power and demonstration of Spirit. He was a devoutly pious and useful minister in his day and time" (Batson, *History of Reedy River Baptist Church*, p. 7).

For nineteen years (1819-1838), Isaac Lamance faithfully labored as Washington's pastor. He was much beloved by the churches he served and well respected and admired by his fellow ministers. In 1839, the Tyger River Baptist Association, meeting that year at Milford, requested that associational churches:

"Send up contributions for the support of Elder
Isaac Lamance who was aged, needy, infirm and
helpless. Elder Samuel Gibson was appointed
agent to take charge of contributions for him, to
procure necessaries for his support, and to report
annually to the association. In response to the
above named request, the churches next year
sent up $134 for the support of Lammence, and
the Association resolved that the request made

last year in regard to him be continued in
the minutes of this meeting, and until, in the
providence of God, there shall seem to be no
further necessity. The churches continued to
send up punctually about $100 every year
for the support of the aged Lammence, and
Gibson continued his faithful and loving agency
until 1847, when death kindly relieved the
old preacher of his earthly wants and the
churches of their earthly charge."
(Griffith, *The Life and Times of
Rev. John G. Landrum*, p. 112).

Lamance's ministry was a time of growth for Washington. J.T. Henerey writes, "During Brother Lamance's pastorate, one hundred and three were baptized, forty-five were received by letter and four were restored to fellowship, making a total of one hundred and forty-eight members. Seventy-two of this number were received from September 1831 to November 1832."

Henerey also relates one episode during Lamance's ministry that is of particular interest. He writes, "I was told by an old friend whose mother attended services regularly at Washington during Bro. Lamance's ministry, that someone had reported Bro. John J. Reynolds to the church for 'patting Jubba' at a corn shucking for a negro to dance. It seemed

" ' Well,' said Bro. Lamance, 'If that's (patting) Jubba, I don't see any great bugaboo in that.' "

that Bro. Lamance did not know what 'patting Jubba' was and no one seemed to be able to explain it so that he could understand, so Bro.

Reynolds got up and said, " 'I'll show you, Bro. Lamance,' and he 'patted Jubba' in the aisle. 'Now', said he, 'that's Jubba.' 'Well,' said Bro. Lamance, 'If that's Jubba, I don't see any great bugaboo in that.' "

Isaac Lamance holds the distinction to this point of being Washington's longest-serving pastor with a tenure of nineteen years. His early work in the church set the tone for evangelism, missions and ministry, which have, since that day, become the hallmarks of our church. A great debt of gratitude is owed to Isaac Lamance, Washington's first pastor.

DENOMINATIONAL AFFILIATIONS

Shortly after its constitution, Washington Baptist Church petitioned for membership in the Broad River Baptist Association. Broad River is one of the oldest Baptist associations in the state of South Carolina, having been organized in 1800. It started with fourteen churches and included congregations as far away as Rutherford County, North Carolina (King, *A History of South Carolina Baptists*, p. 133).

In the minutes of the Broad River Association dated October 13, 1820, it is stated, "Four newly constituted churches have made application for admission into our union and were cordially received, viz: New Prospect, Washington, Crossroads and Macedonia." Washington remained a member of the Broad River Association until 1833, at which time they joined the now defunct Tyger River Baptist Association.

Associational meetings in the old days were quite different from ones today. Sometimes the meetings would last for several days and a variety of issues would be addressed. One important component of nineteenth-century associational gatherings was the teaching and discussion of doctrinal matters. Someone would be appointed by the body the year before to prepare a talk on a matter of doctrinal significance. The next year, that issue would be presented and discussed. Associational meetings were times of education as well as fellowship. Pertinent issues of the day were also commonly discussed. At the 1820 meeting of the Broad River Association — the same year Washington was admitted for membership — the topic discussed was slavery. In those days, slaves were admitted into the membership of white churches. Most churches of that day had galleries, or balconies where slaves would be seated to segregate them from the rest of the congregation — but still, slave and master were in the same building worshiping together.

In October 1820, the question arose, "How shall we proceed with a member that is in slavery, whose companion was taken away by violence, and they have married another? Answer: Agreeably with the Scripture, we cannot hold them in fellowship" (Minutes, Broad River Baptist Association, October 1820).

Washington has continued its associational involvement through the years and has been a member of seven different Baptist associations:

Broad River (1820-1833)
Tyger River (1833-1876) — charter member
Spartanburg (1876-1879)
Greenville (1879-1887)
North Greenville (1887-1959)
Greer (1959-2013) — charter member
Three Rivers (2013 to present) — charter member

THE SOUTH CAROLINA BAPTIST CONVENTION

For some time, Baptists in South Carolina worked together through association, but around the time of Washington's beginning there was a movement afoot in the state to organize a larger, statewide fellowship for the purpose of promoting foreign missions and higher education. Just a few years prior to this, missions pioneer Luther Rice had traveled across South Carolina — informing Baptists of mission efforts in India, and especially the work of Adoniram Judson in Burma, and appealing for financial support. The desire for a better-educated clergy also inspired South Carolina Baptists to invest money and other resources into institutions of higher learning. These issues and others led nine Baptist leaders to meet in Columbia on December 4, 1821, for the express purpose of organizing the South Carolina Baptist Convention. Richard Furman, the dean of South Carolina Baptists at that time, spearheaded the effort. In that initial groundbreaking meeting, a resolution was adopted by the group, stating that "this body do consider their union as founded altogether upon the principles of Gospel truth, Christian affection and liberality; having for their direct object the promotion of the cause and interest of the Redeemer" (King, *A History of South Carolina Baptists*, p. 172). Thus, a statewide movement among Baptists was launched that continues to thrive to this very day.

The desire for a better-educated clergy inspired South Carolina Baptists to invest into institutions of higher learning.

In 1833, under the leadership of Isaac Lamance, Washington Baptist Church became a charter member of the Tyger River Baptist Association. This association appears to have been more sympathetic to state Baptist causes. John G. Landrum — an early leader among upcountry Baptists and the man for whom the town of Landrum was named — was elected the first moderator of the Tyger River Baptist Association, and was one of the original nine organizers of the South Carolina Baptist Convention in 1821. Undoubtedly, Washington became deeply involved in Convention causes when it joined this association. Tyger River Association minutes from that period record:

1838 — Tyger River Association contributed $65.50 for general purposes

1839 — The association contributed $65.41 to foreign missions, with Rev. Samuel Gibson being elected as a delegate to the convention meeting.

(Samuel Gibson became pastor of Washington the following year.)

REV. JESSE CENTER
(1838-1839)

At the conclusion of the long and productive ministry of Rev. Isaac Lamance, Washington extended a pastoral call to their second pastor, Rev. Jesse Center. Center served the church for just one year, from 1838 to 1839. "Elder Center," as he was known, was from the Glassy Mountain area of northern Greenville County. Converted later in life at the age of forty-three, he joined the Head of Tyger Baptist Church and was ordained to the ministry just two years later. Center preached in a number of area churches and was a very effective revival preacher. It has been reported that during a revival he conducted at Glassy Mountain Baptist Church, there were thirty-four conversions, and at another revival he preached at North Fork Church, forty people received Christ. Center was a slaveholder and owned over 1,200 acres of land in the Dark Corner of Greenville County. (McCuen, *Including a Pile of Rocks*, p. 313). It is known that Jesse Center was pastor of Head of Tyger (now Tyger) Baptist Church in 1833. He was a delegate from that church to the organizational meeting of the Tyger River Baptist Association on November 1, 1833. It is unknown whether or not Center came directly from Head of Tyger to Washington in 1838, but it could be safely assumed he did. Around 1846, records show that he was the assistant pastor of Wolf's Creek Baptist Church (now Landrum First). There, he was called to assist their longtime beloved pastor William Harmon, or, as he was affectionately called, "Father Harmon," in his declining years of ministry (Griffith, *The Life and Times of Rev. John G. Landrum*, p. 213).

Brother Center was apparently much loved and respected in the upper part of Greenville County, and called upon to participate not only in religious services, but in civic and patriotic ceremonies as well. In July 1849, the Greenville newspaper reported:

> "On July 4 1849, three or four hundred citizens
> of the Dark Corner met at 'Old Blandenburg' to
> celebrate the Fourth, which was done in patriotic
> style. Captain Moon paraded his uniform
> company. The Company was conducted to the
> stand in the grove. Rev. Jesse Center prayed
> and Captain A.A. Stewart read the
> Declaration of Independence"
> (Batson, *A History of the Upper Part of
> Greenville County, S.C.*, p. 284).

At the time of his death in 1855, Rev. Center was the pastor of Glassy Mountain Baptist Church. At the meeting of the Tyger River Association that year, he was honored and memorialized for his years of faithful service to the kingdom of God (Griffith, *The Life and Times of Rev. John G. Landrum*, p. 118). The papers reported that over 2,000 people attended his funeral at Glassy Mountain Church. Rev. John G. Landrum conducted the service (McCuen, *Including a Pile of Rocks*, p. 313).

A STEP BACK IN TIME

What was Washington Baptist Church like back in the days of Isaac Lamance and Jesse Center? If you were able to travel back in time to the 1830s to worship at Washington, you would find your experience to be much different from what it might be today.

First of all, worship services would be held only one Sunday a month — on each fourth Sunday. On the other three Sundays of the month, your pastor would be preaching elsewhere. Early on in Greenville and Spartanburg counties, there were only a handful of ordained ministers, and they were stretched thin. These dedicated men of God would preach at different churches throughout the month, often traveling for miles on horseback to get to their appointed destination. If your pastor did not live close by, you would likely be boarding him on Saturday night.

On Sunday morning, you would more than likely walk to church. If you did not live within walking distance of the church, you would arrive on horseback, or by buggy or wagon. Modern roads were non-existent. Instead, your route would be a winding, narrow dirt road that would either be dry and dusty during a long dry spell, or wet and muddy when it rained. Whatever the case, if you were clean and neat when you left home for church, by the time you arrived your clothes would either be coated with dust or caked with mud.

Your parking lot would be a grove of trees adjacent to the twin springs that bubble up from the ground, covered with lush undergrowth. Tie your horse to a tall oak tree and walk toward the church. You will soon notice some men gathered together outside the primitive church building, discussing the latest news as they know it. With no televisions, radios or telephones, and very few newspapers, word of mouth is the nineteenth century's most prevalent form of mass communication. As you enter the church building, you are struck by its stark and rustic appearance. It is little more than a log cabin. With only two small windows, those within rely on what little light comes through the door and windows in the spring and summer, and smoky candles scattered here and there in the winter. The ceiling is low. You, being accustomed to a well-lit sanctuary with high ceilings and plenty of windows, are beginning to feel a bit claustrophobic. There are no padded pews in this building, only rough-hewn log benches with no backs. Don't move around too much or you might find a splinter!

If the building is heated at all, it would be a fireplace at one end of the structure. There was no Sunday school prior to worship, because the Sunday school program at Washington didn't arrive until 1873 — nearly forty years later! The pews are divided by an aisle down the middle of the little log church. The men sit on one side, and the women and children sit on the other side. What few deacons there are, would sit together in what would later be known as the "Amen Corner."

> **The pews were divided, with men on one side and women and children on the other.**

This is a very good Sunday. There are twenty-five people in attendance today. There is no idle chatter as the service begins. These people have come to worship. The minister, dressed in his customary black suit with tails descending from the back of the jacket, comes to the front of the small congregation. The solemn expression on his face sets the tone for the service. He climbs onto a low platform that creaks noticeably with every step he takes, and he stands behind a rather plain, unadorned, homemade pulpit that he calls the "bookboard."

After delivering a lengthy opening prayer, he leaves the platform and another brother takes his place. He is the "chorister," and his job is to lead the small company of worshipers in song. The congregation has been introduced to a fairly new and innovative style of singing called "fa-so-la" singing. Later known as "shaped note" music, the songs are acapella with three-part harmony. Once the group finds its pitch, aided by the chorister's tuning fork, they launch into a song with a hauntingly beautiful melody. Spartanburg County native William Walker — or, as he is affectionately known in these parts, "Singing Billy" — has compiled these tunes into a song book he has called "Southern Harmony." Published in 1835, this popular hymnal is a best seller in rural areas of the South. It features a newly composed song by an English clergyman named John Newton. The song has had many titles, but "Singing Billy" chose the title "Amazing Grace." He is not especially happy with any of the tunes that have been applied to it before, so he decides to try another. He selected an old favorite called "New Britain," and, immediately, it's a success. Throughout the South, churches like Washington are singing the song with all their hearts: "Amazing Grace, how sweet the sound that saved a wretch like me. I once was lost, but now I'm found, was blind, but now I see."

"Singing Billy" is in much demand to come to churches to conduct singing schools, teaching the "fa-so-la" method. He's probably even been to Washington at some point. It's an excellent opportunity for him to sell his books. The worshipers heartily sing one song after another. The little log building echoes with heavenly music.

You look behind you, and you see a small group of slaves huddled together in the back of the little building. They are encouraged by their masters to come to church. When the singing stops, the congregation is seated and a bag is passed from bench to bench. The collection is small today. Nobody has any money to give. What they can give, they give gladly.

Once again, the pastor ascends the platform and lays his big, black, bulky Bible upon the pulpit, opened to the text for the day. In loud, clear tones he reverently reads God's Word, and then ceremoniously closes the book. He falls to his knees and prays another long, eloquent prayer. "Amens" resound throughout the tiny building. When the pastor closes his prayer, he rises slowly and begins his sermon. The preacher has very little formal education, but he can read — and he has spent many a night, after he has completed his farm chores, sitting by candlelight, reading what few books he could afford. He is well-versed in the scriptures, and to his faithful church that's all that really matters. He preaches from the heart, and with tears. His sermon begins slowly at first, but like an old locomotive, he gathers steam. His pace quickens, and soon he is carrying his listeners to the very gates of Zion! There is much emotion in the service. Frequent cries of "amen," "hallelujah," and "praise the Lord" can be heard during the preacher's lengthy discourse.

Finally, after only an hour, a short sermon according to the standards of that day, the message is brought to a close. The tired, perspiring preacher steps aside and a deacon comes to the front. This brother has the "gift of exhortation." Today we would call it "extending the invitation," but the exhorter's job is to bring the service to a close, and, by the power of the Holy Spirit, bring people to a decision. First one comes, then another. One by one, repentant sinners kneel at the front of the makeshift chapel. One brother who faces exclusion from the church begs for forgiveness and restoration. Another professes faith in Christ and will soon be baptized in Beaver Dam Creek, where it runs through Berry's pasture.

After many tears and embraces, the service concludes. You know you have been to church, but you are ready to reenter your time machine and come back to the twenty-first century. You still miss your air-conditioned sanctuary and padded pew.

REV. SAMUEL GIBSON
(1840-1843 and 1853-1854)

Rev. Samuel Gibson

In June 1840, Washington Baptist Church extended the pastoral call to one of the most well-known and beloved ministers of his day, Rev. Samuel Gibson. Gibson began his tenure at Washington on June 27, 1840, and served faithfully until June 1843. He briefly served as pastor for a second time for one year in 1853. During Gibson's ministry at Washington, six were received by baptism, nine by letter, and one was restored to fellowship (Henerey, p. 5).

Samuel Gibson was born in Woolwich, England, on April 1, 1779. At the age of twenty, he was converted and joined a Baptist church. Soon after his conversion, he felt the call to preach and began preaching in Baptist assemblies around London. Gibson was actively involved in England's early Sunday school movement, and leaders of his class were so impressed with the young preacher's abilities, integrity and strength of character that they raised money to send him to school for four years. After this, he was soon ordained to the Gospel ministry. He and his wife, Elizabeth, and Elizabeth's sister decided to come to America and arrived in New York in either 1815 or 1817. Shortly after arriving in New York, Gibson and his family made their way to Charleston. They were penniless and friendless, yet full of faith and vision.

Soon after their arrival in Charleston, they quickly found the Baptist church and went there to worship on their first Sunday in the city. The story goes that the church's chorister was having difficulty that morning "raising a tune" for the congregation's first hymn. After a couple of failed attempts and an embarrassing silence in the church, Samuel Gibson arose, found the pitch perfectly, and then, with his wife and sister-in-law joining in, sang the hymn beautifully. The church was deeply moved by their presentation and immediately fell in love with the English trio. Pastor and people begged the Gibsons to remain among them, even offering to find the young preacher employment. When they discovered Gibson was a blacksmith by trade, they negotiated with him to repair the church's bell, which had been out of use for some time. When he successfully repaired the bell, they tried to give him ten dollars, but he would only accept two.

In spite of the Baptist church's plea for the Gibsons to remain in Charleston, the adventurous English preacher wished to move further into the interior of South Carolina, which, at that time, was still largely unpopulated and wild. Moving into the upper reaches of Greenville County, both Samuel and Elizabeth were struck by the wickedness and void of Christian influence that were prevalent on the frontier at that time. Drunkenness, sexual immorality, murder and all sorts of other mischief were the order of the day. Elizabeth reportedly lamented to her husband, "The harvest is ready and there is no laborer to reap it."

Early on, Samuel Gibson became associated with Reedy River Baptist Church. He acquired land in that section and served as Reedy River's pastor on two separate occasions, 1819-1826 and 1842-1846. However, it soon became apparent that Gibson's influence would be widespread. He served a number of Baptist churches in the upper part of South Carolina — with his greatest influence being felt at Milford Baptist Church, where he served the longest, and where he and Elizabeth are buried in the church cemetery.

Samuel Gibson, like most ministers in Greenville County at that time, was stretched thin because of ever-increasing preaching duties and responsibilities. It is said that there were times when he would be so ill or weary that he could barely pull himself up out of bed to go preach at his next appointment. More than once, his beloved wife, Elizabeth, would encourage him, "Go on, Sammy, a good pulpit sweat will cure you!"

> **"Go on, Sammy, a good pulpit sweat will cure you!"**

There would be no way of knowing how many hundreds of thousands of miles Samuel Gibson and his contemporaries traveled to preach the Gospel, often to only a handful of people. Professor H.P. Griffith, an early president of Limestone College and author of *The Life and Times of Rev. John G. Landrum* (which I have frequently cited in this book), reminisced:

> "Well does the author remember, when a little boy, to have gazed with childish wonder, mingled with awe, upon a little red-faced old man, with white hair, scrupulously neat in his dress and peculiarly solemn in his appearance, seated in a sulky and driving a snow-white horse rapidly toward a neighboring church; and well does he remember how that wonder was increased and that awe deepened, when he noted the death-like stillness that reigned in the congregation as he ascended the pulpit, and saw the trembling of strong men and gay women under the power of his soul-stirring words."

Griffith is offering here a detailed description of Samuel Gibson and a firsthand account of his powerful pulpit ministry.

Rev. Samuel Gibson was a strong advocate for missions and education, and was actively involved in associational work as well as the work of the South Carolina Baptist Convention. Associational records of the day state that he made frequent appeals for the funding of Furman University. He also, at one point, was employed by the South Carolina Baptist Convention to travel across the state to promote convention causes and receive monies for its support. On December 6, 1825, the Baptist state convention took the following action: "Appointed Rev. Samuel Gibson Domestic Missionary and Agent, to travel and preach within the limits of this State; with the view particularly, of soliciting contributions, and subscriptions, in aid of the institutions, and of the other important designs of the body: agreed that his compensation be $400, for the year, or $500, if the funds at the end of the year will allow it. The president to furnish him with credentials and instructions" (King, *A History of South Carolina Baptists*, p. 224).

After a long and productive ministry, Samuel Gibson was called to his heavenly reward on December 5, 1857. His headstone at Milford is inscribed with the following:

> "Sacred to the memory of Rev. Samuel Gibson.
> Born in Woolwich, England, April 1779.
> Died December 5, 1857. Aged 78 years."

At the meeting of the Tyger River Association the next year, the body mourned the passing of:

> "Elder Samuel Gibson, who had been gathered
> to his people like a ripe shock into the garner.

He was a self-made man, an able minister
of the New Testament — eloquent, forcible,
and faithful — a minister of great purity
of character, sustaining in private life an
unblemished Christian reputation."

Rev. Samuel Gibson left behind many descendants who, even today, serve the churches in which they are involved with the same dedication and commitment as their distinguished ancestor.

(This biographical information was taken from H.P. Griffith's *Life and Times of Rev. John G. Landrum*, pp. 101-103; pp. 119-120. Also, Mann Batson's *A History of the Upper Part of Greenville County, S.C.*, pp. 201-202.)

Following Samuel Gibson's ministry at Washington, Rev. W.T. Crane served briefly. He came in June of 1843 and left that December. Little is known about Crane other than the fact that, according to Henerey, he was licensed to the ministry by Pleasant Hill Baptist Church.

Church records from the 1840s indicate that Washington went through some lean times in these early days. For example, the church reported to the Tyger River Association that in 1844 there were no deacons at Washington. There was not a church clerk, and there was only one male member — Asa Cunningham. The clerk of the association that year commented in the association's minutes, "This was once a large and flourishing body, but many have been dismissed to form new churches. Her present number is thirty-two" (Tyger River Associational Minutes, 1844). The absence of church records from these days makes

In 1844, there were no deacons and only one male member at Washington.

it impossible to speculate as to why the church experienced this downswing in attendance and activity. If internal problems were brewing at this time, we would have no way of knowing the nature or scope of these difficulties. Fortunately, Washington was able, as she always has been down through the years with the help of the Lord, to overcome the challenges she faced and soon prosper and flourish once again.

And so the first twenty-five years of Washington Baptist Church's existence comes to a close with a small group of people, low in number, but high in faith. The days ahead are looking up!

—— | Chapter Three | ——
DAYS OF TURBULENCE
1845-1870

The decade of the 1840s was a busy and important time for the people of Washington Baptist Church, and, indeed, for the young nation of the United States of America. America was beginning to flex its muscles as a world player and was starting to realize what would later be called its "Manifest Destiny."

Down in the new Republic of Texas, American settlers were being regularly attacked and harassed by Mexican forces under the infamous General Santa Anna. The American Army was sent in to lend support and protection to the citizens of Texas, but they, too, were soon attacked by the Mexicans, prompting President James K. Polk to declare war on Mexico April 25, 1846. Palmetto state volunteers were among the first to enlist for battle. Two area battalions served with distinction: the Saluda Volunteers and the Tyger Volunteers, both raised in June 1846. No doubt, some young men from the Washington community volunteered for service.

On Monday, September 13, 1847, a major stronghold was taken that would hasten the end of the war. The Castle Chapultec (the legendary Hall of Montezuma from Marine Corps fame) was taken by American forces led by South Carolina volunteers. The American flag was raised over the conquered fortress and then, almost simultaneously, the Palmetto flag of South Carolina was raised to fly alongside Old Glory to honor the bravery of the South Carolinians who first stormed the castle. The Mexican War came to a close in February 1848, and triumphant South Carolina soldiers returned to their homes and their farms. Texas was finally secured, and later, many from South Carolina would move there looking for greater opportunity.

> Another role in Washington's history was the formation of the Southern Baptist Convention in May of 1845.

Another historic and monumental event took place in 1845 that would play a profound role in the history of Washington Baptist Church, and that was the formation of the Southern Baptist Convention in May of 1845.

Prior to 1845, the Baptists of America were united into one body known as the Triennial Convention because it met once every three years. The major thrust of this group was foreign missions, particularly the support of Adoniram Judson in Burma. Under the growing influence of Northeast abolitionists the Triennial Convention decided to withhold its endorsement of missionaries who were slaveholders. The controversy all came to a head in 1844 when the Home Mission Society refused to ordain James E. Reeve of Georgia as a missionary because he owned slaves.

As a result of this decision by the Triennial Convention, Baptists from the South met together in Augusta, Georgia, in May of 1845 and formed what would become known as the Southern Baptist Convention, for the purpose of mutual support and fellowship and the support of foreign missions. Washington's early involvement in the Southern Baptist Convention is largely unknown because of poor recordkeeping, but one could naturally assume the church financially supported the convention's first mission endeavors. Mission support has long been an important hallmark of Washington. As far as we know, the first Washington pastor to attend the Southern Baptist Convention as a delegate of the North Greenville Baptist Association was Rev. J.R. Aiken, who served the church from 1888 to 1892.

REV. RICHARD WOODRUFF
(1844-1847, 1852-1853, 1854-1857)

Rev. Richard Woodruff

Rev. Richard Woodruff served as pastor of Washington on three separate occasions, the first beginning on October 26, 1844. Woodruff was ordained to the ministry by Clear Springs Baptist Church on May 28, 1837 (Langford, *A Stroll Through* ... , p. 12). During his twelve years at Washington, thirty people were baptized and fifteen were received by letter (Henerey).

In later life it was written of Woodruff, "He retains many of the peculiarities of an eventful ministerial life, and still loves to talk of a Savior's dying love, and to persuade sinners to repent. He is a man of a warm heart and deep, earnest piety, and, but for constitutional eccentricities of disposition, would have been a widely useful man (Griffith, *The Life and Times of Rev. John G. Landrum,* p. 175). One can only imagine what was meant by his "constitutional eccentricities of disposition."

REV. JEFFERSON BARTON
(1848-1850)

Jefferson Barton was a native of the upper part of Greenville County and was the son of Revolutionary War veteran David Barton and his wife, Nancy Barrett Barton. He, along with another future Washington pastor, Jesse Center, was converted to Christianity at Tyger Baptist Church in 1832. And then in 1834, both Center and Barton were ordained to the Gospel ministry on the same day. They were, in fact, ordained by another Washington pastor, Rev. Isaac Lamance.

Jefferson Barton, in addition to Washington, served Brushy Creek, Milford and Mountain Creek churches. During Barton's ministry at Washington, three were baptized and five were received by letter. Shortly after leaving Washington, Barton and his family moved to Georgia, and then on to Arkansas, where he died in 1862. His body was carried back to Canton, Georgia, where he was buried.

In a brief biographical sketch from the minutes of the Tyger River Baptist Association, Rev. Barton was characterized as a:

"Clear headed, sensible man, possessing natural talents far above the majority of men in his day. He was a close, compact, pointed and forcible speaker, dexterous and shrewd in debate, and generally had the good fortune to be on the right side. He was a successful and much beloved minister of the Gospel. His character was of the

positive and not of the negative kind. He boldly
defended the truth, and proclaimed war
against drunkenness, vice and immorality"
(McCuen, *Including a Pile of Rocks*,
pp. 453-456).

REV. RICHARD WEBB
(1850-1852)

Richard Webb, or as he is often called, Elder Webb, served as Washington's pastor for two years, beginning in February 1850. An Englishman by birth, he also served Brushy Creek and Pleasant Grove Churches simultaneous to the time he was at Washington. There are no existing records of his time at Washington, but we are aware of a great revival meeting that he preached at Brushy Creek in August of 1850, during which twenty-four were converted to Christ, one came into the church by letter, and one was restored to fellowship (Kahl, *The Bicentennial History of Brushy Creek Baptist Church*, pp. 52 and 70).

After Elder Webb's departure, some former pastors returned to serve briefly. Richard Woodruff and Samuel Gibson both served the church from 1852 until the beginning of S.T. Dill's lengthy pastorate in 1858.

REV. S.T. DILL
(1858-1865, 1884-1886)

S.T. Dill was a much-beloved pastor who had served Tyger Baptist Church and lived in the Tigerville area, where he had a store for several years.

"Churches of the Baptist persuasion are numerous about here: but the one that the people of this place are wont to attend is called the Head of Tyger, where your and my beloved friend, Rev. S.T. Dill, tells the Gospel truths. All the members of his flock are much attached to him, and richly he deserves their esteem" (Batson, *A History of the Upper Part of South Carolina*, p. 30, quoting *The Enterprise and Mountaineer* newspaper from December 12, 1883).

Dill married a daughter of Rev. Samuel Gibson and pastored Washington on two separate occasions — 1858-1865 and 1884-1886. It was during Dill's ministry that Washington built a new and larger house of worship. J.T. Henerey writes, "In May 1858, the church began the erection of a large house 40x60 feet. Brethren Asa Cunningham, W.D. Berry, R.J. Foster, Henry S. Gibson and J.K. Dickson were the building committee. Bro. Gibson was a member of Milford, and Bro. J.K. Dickson a member of Mt. Tabor, a Presbyterian church. The building was not completed until sometime after the war, and was never dedicated, as far as I am able to learn."

Rev. S.T. Dill evidently had a successful ministry at Washington, with the congregation growing to the point that a larger building was required. And so well esteemed was he by the church that he was invited to return and minister to the flock on a second occasion: March 1884 to December 1886. During his combined terms of service at Washington, there were eighty-five additions by baptism, twenty-two by letter, and two restored to fellowship.

'A GREAT CIVIL WAR'

Tensions between the North and the South really began in 1833 with the so-called "Nullification Crisis." In 1828, a protective tariff was approved by Congress to aid the industrial machine of the North, but in so doing it did great harm to the Southern economy. South Carolina, believing that, as a sovereign state, they had the right to nullify the tariff, was threatened by President Andrew Jackson with military intervention if they did not comply. A compromise was reached and the crisis passed, but hard feelings between Northerners and Southerners remained. Divisions grew deeper with every passing year, especially over the issue of slavery. Northern abolitionists fought hard to end the practice of slavery, but not without great political resistance from Southern politicians. The struggle came to a dramatic conclusion with the creation of the abolitionist Republican party, the presidential candidacy of Abraham Lincoln, and Lincoln's election to the presidency on November 6, 1860.

On December 20, 1860, 170 men representing different regions of South Carolina and different walks of life met in Columbia and signed the historic Ordinance of Secession, declaring South Carolina's sovereign independence from the United States of America. One of the signers was, in fact, Rev. John G. Landrum, the much-esteemed Baptist minister who pastored so many churches in our area.

On April 12, 1861, Fort Sumter was fired upon by forces under the command of General

In 1861, many brave men in our church and community heeded the call and fought under the Confederate battle flag during the Civil War.

P.G.T. Beauregard, and with that first shot the Civil War began. By the time the conflict ended in 1865, nearly 1 million Americans would have lost their lives. It was America's darkest hour. Undoubtedly, many brave men in the church and the Washington community heeded the call to service and fought under the Confederate battle flag.

For the most part, men in the area would have fought for the Sixteenth Regiment of Volunteers. The soldiers of this regiment were involved in some of the bloodiest fighting of the War in the western theater of operation in Tennessee. The Sixteenth's heaviest losses were sustained at the Battle of Franklin near Nashville. The first person buried in the cemetery at Washington Baptist Church was Captain R.J. Foster, who was an officer in Company D of the Sixteenth Regiment.

The war finally came to an end in April 1865, and the men of Washington returned to their homes, their farms and their church, but the scars of war remained for many years.

REV. T.J. EARLE
(1866-1867)

Rev. T.J. Earle

One of the most widely respected and honored ministers and educators in South Carolina, Rev. Thomas Jefferson Earle, served Washington briefly as pastor in the years following the Civil War.

The Earles were early settlers in Greenville County and one of the most distinguished families in the area, producing ministers, physicians, attorneys, politicians, college professors and college presidents.

Born in Landrum, South Carolina on December 23, 1824, T.J. Earle graduated from Mercer University in Macon, Georgia. Soon after graduation, he was ordained to the Gospel ministry at New Prospect Baptist Church in Spartanburg County, South Carolina on May 23, 1852. Dr. J.C. Furman preached his ordination sermon, and Rev. John G. Landrum was a participant in the service. Earle served a number of churches simultaneously — his longest pastorate being Gowensville Baptist Church, where he served from 1856 until his death on August 6, 1889. He is buried at Gowensville Church cemetery, and his impressive monument is inscribed with these words:

"He simply, wisely, lovingly, earnestly, powerfully
told us of Jesus. The sinner's friend"
(Howard, *Dark Corner Heritage*, pp. 30-31).

Perhaps Earle's greatest work, however, was done outside the church in the field of education. In 1858, he opened the Gowensville Seminary, attracting students from all over the state of South Carolina. This quality institution of learning offered a classical education to young men and women alike. In 1869, it was reported that the seminary had enrolled fifty-five students (Howard, *Dark Corner Heritage*, p. 29).

Rev. Earle's home, "Earlesdale," still stands to this day and is located about a mile north of Gowensville First Baptist Church on South Carolina Highway 14. The beautiful, two-story, red brick home is still a private residence, but during Earle's time it doubled as his residence and a dormitory for his school's students. It's said that originally the upstairs of the home had a divider in the hall to segregate the boys from the girls. Rev. Earle ran a strict school.

Washington considered it an honor to have secured the services of Rev. Earle for the brief time he was there. It is recorded that during Earle's ministry, one member was added by baptism and eleven came by letter.

REV. M.V.B. LANKFORD
(1868-1870)

Fifty years of Washington history came to a close in 1869 during the ministry of Rev. Martin Van Buren Lankford. Rev. Lankford was a native of Rutherford County, North Carolina, and studied at the Davidson Academy (Langford, *A Stroll Through* ... , p. 16).

Little is known about Rev. Lankford or his time at Washington, other than the fact that during his two-year tenure, eight were received by baptism and one by letter.

———┤ Chapter Four ├———

A FIRM FOUNDATION
1871-1896

As the year 1871 dawned, Washington Baptist Church continued to grow and thrive as a great community witness. And yet times were still difficult, particularly for the South. The so-called Reconstruction Era was a thirteen-year period following the Civil War when the South was basically under martial law. A strong military presence was in Greenville County at this time to ensure that post-war laws were enforced, particularly in regard to the newly freed slaves. Ex-slaves were in a dilemma of sorts. They enjoyed freedom, but most of them really had nowhere to go. Former slave owners, sympathetic to their plight, retained many of them as farm hands and tried to lend them support, even though many of them were destitute themselves. Local government was under the control of recently arrived Northerners, who soon came to be called "carpetbaggers" because the luggage they carried was made of a carpet-like material.

Though times were tough, life continued on as normally as possible around Washington Baptist Church. The faithful remained true to the services and ministries of the church during these difficult days. The doors remained open.

REV. RICHARD FURMAN WHILDEN
(1870, 1876)

Rev. Richard Furman Whilden

R.F. Whilden was one of the most intriguing and colorful of all of Washington's pastors during this early period. A native of Charleston, Whilden must have boasted some aristocratic Charlestonian roots. He was a product of the historic First Baptist Church of Charleston, the first Baptist church in the South. It was at this church that Whilden was licensed and ordained to the ministry. He received his education at the College of Charleston (Langford, *Pastors of Washington Baptist Church*, p. 4). After graduation, he spent time as a tutor for a number of prominent lowcountry families.

What brought him to the Upstate is unknown, but he soon settled in and made his mark.

John Weaver, prominent local businessman and owner of Weaver Mill (later Berry's Mill), died in 1862. His widow, Martha, was a granddaughter of Rev. Samuel Gibson. In 1864, she married R.F. Whilden. Whilden signed a prenuptial agreement, agreeing not to "intermeddle in any part of the rents, issues and profits of the real estate" (Batson, *Water Powered Gristmills and Their Owners*, p. 168). Soon, however, Weaver

Factory had been renamed Whilden Factory. And in true Charlestonian fashion, R.F. Whilden named the rambling two-story home across from the mill "Whilden Hall."

From the Greenville newspaper, *The Enterprise and Mountaineer* of October 1, 1884, we read:

> "Upon leaving O'neal, after proceeding a few miles, we came to the place formerly known as Weaver's Factory. It was afterwards known as Whilden's Hall. Here the late John Weaver built and established a cotton factory, which he conducted with success for many years. Mr. Weaver died about 1862. It is our recollection that the premises were robbed by bushwhackers about the time the war closed. In the meantime his widow had married R.F. Whilden, a gentleman of education and culture from Charleston, and a minister of the Gospel who kept the factory in operation for several years after the cessation of hostilities between the States, but now is suspended and the machinery has been moved away" (Batson, *Water Powered Gristmills and Their Owners,* p. 169).

Whilden preached in other area churches in addition to his role as businessman and country squire. He returned to Washington to serve as pastor for one year in 1876. Whilden and his wife had seven children together. Martha died April 8, 1880, at the age of forty-three, and R.F. died February 4, 1905. Both are buried in the Milford Baptist Church cemetery. During Whilden's pastorate at Washington, two were received by letter.

REV. A.D. BOWERS
(1871)

Rev. A.D. Bowers

Following Whilden's brief ministry, another colorful and much-loved pastor served Washington for one year, beginning in 1871. He was the Rev. Alexander D. Bowers.

Born in 1846, he was licensed to preach on July 2, 1859, by Glassy Mountain Baptist Church. He was later ordained to the Gospel ministry at Glassy Mountain on June 10, 1861. During his long and illustrious career, he pastored twenty-three churches and was instrumental in the organization of Oak Grove, Locust Hill, Highland, Camp Creek and Ebenezer Welcome. Bowers served as moderator of the North Greenville Association in 1893 and 1894.

Two stories best illustrate the courageous and dedicated character of A.D. Bowers. A Confederate veteran, Bowers saw firsthand what effect alcohol was having on war veterans who returned home and turned to the bottle to deal with the horrors they had experienced on the battlefield. Of course, a lot of corn whiskey was being distilled in the Dark Corner section of northern Greenville County where Bowers lived and preached. He became an outspoken critic of blockade whiskey, and in doing so he aroused the anger of local moonshiners. They began to openly threaten the preacher with death. One Sunday morning as Bowers stood to preach, some of his sworn enemies showed up at the church and stuck the barrels of their guns through the open windows, with the intention of killing Bowers while he preached. Reportedly, he stopped his sermon and spoke directly to his would-be assassins, saying, "God has given me a message to

> **"God has given me a message to preach. Just wait until I finish preaching it, then you can kill me."**

preach. Just wait until I finish preaching it, then you can kill me." Bowers' courage made such an impression on the men that they withdrew their guns and left the scene without incident.

Another favorite story involves a group of Mormon missionaries who were camping in the Highland community with the intention of proselytizing the local residents. The old Baptist preacher supposedly sent word to the missionaries that if they didn't leave the community immediately, he would "set some fellows on them." They wisely took the threat seriously and were out of the Dark Corner by sundown.

Records indicate that during Bowers' ministry at Washington, four joined the church by letter.

A.D. Bowers died on February 2, 1909, and he and his wife are buried in the cemetery of Highland Baptist Church. In the 1909 annual meeting of the North Greenville Baptist Association, a page of the minutes was dedicated to the memory of A.D. Bowers because, as the one who made the motion said:

"You all know, our dear Brother Bowers wore
out his life laboring in the cause of our
Master and for the salvation of souls"
(Howard, *Dark Corner Heritage*, pp. 62-63).

REV. JASON C. HUDSON
(1872-1875)

Rev. Jason C. Hudson

Little information can be found about Jason C. Hudson, but his ministry at Washington was noteworthy for two reasons.

First, it seems there was a real emphasis on mission support during his days at the church. J.T. Henerey writes, "During the period beginning with 1873 to the present time (1901), the church commenced taking collections every meeting for missions, and by referring to the minutes of the association you will see what progress has been made along this line."

Another landmark event occurred during Hudson's ministry in 1872. The first burial took place on church property when Captain R.J. Foster was laid to rest in the churchyard. Foster was a Confederate veteran and an officer in the Sixteenth South Carolina Volunteers. He was also a deacon and leader at Washington. His grave is easy to identify, because it is out of line from the other graves. As was noted earlier, William Berry, who first donated land to the church, reportedly stipulated that there be no burials on the property for fear that it might foul his twin

Captain R.J. Foster, 1822-1872. A former Washington deacon and superintendent of Sunday school, he was also the first to be buried in the Washington cemetery.

springs. Following his death in 1872, his son evidently didn't share his father's fear and thus permitted the burial of Captain Foster. After that, people have continuously been buried in the Washington cemetery for 176 years. Currently there are 1,411 plots in the graveyard. As in most old church cemeteries, identification of many of the oldest graves are impossible because field stones were originally used to mark the graves and over the years these rocks may have been moved, lost or destroyed.

The Washington Baptist cemetery is, indeed, a sacred spot for us all. It has been well maintained by the church and families over the years, and is a good place to walk and meditate on a beautiful day. Ancient grave stone inscriptions are interesting to read, and many of the old tombstones are works of art. There's much history to be learned there. There are also tragic tales to be told. For example, a long line of tiny markers in one plot tells the story of a family who lost a number of children on successive days due to some deadly disease that passed through these parts. This is our hallowed ground.

It was also during this period in 1876 that W.D. Berry Jr. deeded four acres to the church, which is a part of our present property. Washington paid just $19.50 for the four acres, an outstanding price even for that day (Langford, *A Stroll Through* ... , p. 5).

By the time Rev. Hudson completed his ministry at Washington he had left his mark with these important events taking place during his tenure. In addition, eighteen people were added to the rolls of the church — nine by baptism and nine by letter.

Rev. R.F. Whilden returned briefly to lead the church after Hudson left in 1876.

REV. LUDWELL VAUGHAN
(1877-1883)

Rev. Ludwell Vaughan

Ludwell Vaughan was converted to Christ on July 18, 1854, during an eleven-day revival meeting at Brushy Creek Baptist Church in Taylors. He later joined Pleasant Grove Baptist Church in Greer and was ordained to the ministry there in 1857. He had very little formal education, but he applied himself to learn all he could and became a very popular pastor and preacher in the area. In addition to Washington, Vaughan also served Brushy Creek, Pleasant Grove, Fairview and Greer First Baptist churches.

Ludwell Vaughan died on July 18, 1899, and along with his wife, Sallie, is buried in the Pleasant Grove Baptist Church cemetery. The annual minutes of the South Carolina Baptist Convention for the year 1899 contains the obituary of Rev. Ludwell Vaughan and says:

> "This estimable brother died at Greer, Greenville
> County, July 18, aged seventy-seven years.
> He labored faithfully as a minister of
> Jesus Christ, mainly in Greenville County,
> and his labors were signally blessed in the
> conversion of souls. He died as he had lived,
> very greatly beloved and respected for
> his Christian character"
> (Kahl, *The Bicentennial History of
> Brushy Creek Baptist Church*, p. 74).

Vaughan's time at Washington was a period of great growth. Thirty were baptized into the kingdom, and fifteen were received by letter.

Another former pastor, Rev. S.T. Dill, returned to Washington following Vaughan's departure. He served from 1884 to 1886. During this time, records show that two were baptized and ten were added by letter. And the Lord continued to add to His church!

REV. JESSE M. ALLEN
(1887)

Washington's next pastor, Rev. Jesse M. Allen, served briefly for just one year. One joined the church by letter that year. No reason is given for the brevity of his tenure.

REV. P.D. GREEN
(1888)

Once again, another pastorate is noted for its brevity. P.D. Green received the call to serve Washington after the departure of Jesse Allen. Little is known about Rev. Green other than the fact that he was a product of Brushy Creek Baptist Church in Taylors, and had been ordained as a deacon there in 1887 (Kahl, *The Bicentennial History of Brushy Creek Baptist Church*, p. 66). During that year of ministry at Washington, Green baptized eleven people. Also of note, in the year 1888, Washington's first historian, J.T. Henerey, began serving as church clerk. It was also in the year 1888 that Washington quit the practice of the annual call for the pastor. Up to this point, the pastor was elected every year, but that changed in 1888 — much to the relief of the generations of Washington pastors, who would later come on the scene.

REV. J.R. AIKEN
(1888-1892)

Rev. J.R. Aiken was born on October 23, 1861, in Gowensville, South Carolina. In his youth, he attended Earle's Seminary and then went on to Furman University and the Southern Baptist Theological Seminary in Louisville, Kentucky (Langford, *A Stroll Through* ..., p. 21). During his time at Washington, Aiken also served Gowensville and Taylors First churches.

In the 1889 associational minutes, it was reported that the value of Washington's property was $500. Church membership was counted at 145. Twenty-five had been baptized that year, with two joining by letter.

Rev. J.R. Aiken

One hundred sixty-five were enrolled in Washington's Sunday school that year. Sunday school had played an important role in the church since it had been established back in 1840.

In 1892, records indicated that Pastor Aiken was living in Fairforest, perhaps serving the Baptist church there at the same time he was pastoring Washington. Aiken left Washington Baptist Church in 1892 and eventually moved to Greenville, where he died in 1925 at the age of sixty-four.

We have this event from J.R. Aiken's time:

"Henry S. Gibson died at his home near Washington church on Monday the 22nd ult. On Wednesday preceding he was paralyzed throughout the whole of his right side and was not able to talk. He was seventy-five years of age. He was born in London, England, and crossed the ocean when only a year old, landing in Charleston; his family afterwards moving to this section. During his long life he never bought a bushel of corn or a bushel of wheat, except in 1846, the year after the dry year, and then only seed of those cereals. He leaves two children, Mrs. Sallie Ponder and James Gibson, and his wife also survives him. He was

buried at Washington church. Rev. J.R. Aiken
conducted the funeral services"
(Batson, *A History of the Upper Part of
Greenville County, S.C.,* p. 119).

REV. J.L. FREEMAN
(1893-1895)

In January 1893, J.L. Freeman, a native of Pickens County, was called to be Washington's eighteenth pastor. A recent graduate of Furman University, he served the church with a youthful enthusiasm that won over many followers. During his two years of ministry at Washington, thirty-nine were baptized, eleven were received by letter, and two were restored to fellowship. Desiring to complete his ministerial education, Freeman left Washington to pursue his studies at the Southern Baptist Theological Seminary in Louisville, Kentucky.

Rev. D.P. Montgomery

REV. D.P. MONTGOMERY
(1895-1896)

Upon J.L. Freeman's departure, the church issued a pastoral call to Rev. David Pressley Montgomery of Lancaster County, South Carolina. A graduate of Furman University and the Southern Baptist Theological Seminary, Montgomery took over a church that now had a membership of 218. The value of the church property, according to associational records, was now up to a whopping $800, and the reported capacity of their house of worship was 550. The pastor's annual salary was now $125 a year. Rev. Montgomery was a delegate of the church to the Southern Baptist Convention in 1896.

When D.P. Montgomery completed his ministry at Washington in December 1896, he had baptized nine and the church had received two by letter.

—| Chapter Five |—
A NEW CENTURY
1897-1919

The new year of 1897 began with Washington searching for their twentieth pastor. The Lord would certainly bless their efforts by bringing a man of God who was well loved by the congregation.

REV. J.E. McMANAWAY
(1897-1908)

J.E. McManaway was a native of Chamblissburg, Virginia. He graduated from Wake Forest College with honors and later attended the Southern Baptist Theological Seminary. Ordained by Tryon Street Baptist Church in Charlotte, North Carolina, he came to Greer from Chester, South Carolina. He served Washington, Pleasant Grove, and Greer First Baptist simultaneously. His ministry at all three churches was productive and notable. He was widely loved in the city of Greer and the surrounding countryside, and the feeling was mutual. He once wrote, "If you live in Greer long enough to see the leaves bud and fall from the trees, you will

Rev. J.E. McManaway

never want to leave." Many of us can share that sentiment!

In his shared ministry between the three churches, he divided his preaching and pastoral duties by preaching at Greer First two Sundays a month, and then one Sunday a month for both Washington and Pleasant Grove.

McManaway's pastorate at Washington was a time of growth. When he came to the church in 1897, the church officially recorded a membership of 191. By the time he left in January 1908, the membership was at 237. There were ninety-two baptisms during his years of ministry at Washington.

It was during McManaway's ministry that the church determined a need for a larger place of worship. On July 31, 1899, ground was broken for the third sanctuary that Washington would occupy up to that point. As of May 1901, $1,300 had been spent on the construction (Henerey). The building was dedicated to the Lord on May 18, 1901, and at the time of its construction it faced Bomar Road. It was hoped that a baptistry could be added to the building, but it would be many years before an indoor baptistry would be installed. Located in the area that is now the front church parking lot, the baptistry was outdoors and remained there until at least the 1950s.

There's another interesting story that goes along with the construction of the sanctuary, and it's regarding the church bell. When the new building was being discussed, Mr. Spartan Commodore Berry told the group that if a belfry was built in the new church, he would donate a bell. Some of the members, according to the story, suggested that they

The Washington bell, 1901.

form a committee to find a "good bell," maybe suspecting that Mr. Berry might cut corners purchasing the bell. Mr. Berry assured the church that if he bought it, it *would* be a good bell. And he did — and it was!

In fact, the bell was rung every Sunday from 1901 until 1964, when it was finally retired. It now resides next to the prayer chapel and is still rung on very special occasions.

A letter Rev. McManaway wrote to *The Baptist Courier* on May 23, 1901, reveals the humor of this well-loved pastor. He wrote:

"In looking through the old records of Washington
church I found where the church retired two of
her deacons after only one year of service, giving
as a reason that they were not 'ripe.' Now I know
what is the matter with some of the deacons of
some of our Baptist churches — they are not
ripe. They were pulled too soon."

Rev. McManaway was also known for his passionate preaching. It was said about his final sermon as pastor of Pleasant Grove:

"The service was powerful and spirited. The
pastor preached from the text, 'My Master
calleth thee.' The sermon, I think, was the most
powerful I have ever heard. Never have I seen
a congregation so deeply moved. Hoary headed
men and women wept like children. Men and
women who were just passing the noontide of
life: young men and young ladies, robust and
strong in intellect and emotion — all yielded to
the magnetic influence of the pastor, which he
had built up during his pastorate, and wept
as though their hearts would break."

Undoubtedly, the people at Washington shared this same kind of sadness when McManaway's ministry here came to a conclusion somewhere near the end of 1907. His eleven years at Washington were years of growth and progress. In later years, J.E. McManaway would move to Greenville and become a field editor for *The Baptist Courier*. He died in Greenville on February 28, 1930 (information on J.E. McManaway

*This Lord's Supper service set was purchased for the church by
Mr. Broadus Carlisle Berry, father of Mrs. Lola Berry Barnett.
The set was used in the 1800s and early 1900s. Members who took
communion drank from the same cup.*

taken from Kinard, *A Strong Tower,* pp. 48-61).

Rev. Harry Lee Riley

REV. HARRY LEE RILEY
(1908-1910)

Early in the year of 1908, Washington welcomed her next pastor, Rev. Harry Lee Riley. Once again, they were sharing a pastor with Greer First Baptist Church, as they had with Rev. McManaway.

Riley was born in Martinsburg, West Virginia, on June 24, 1872. He, like so many other early Washington pastors, was graduated from Furman University and the Southern Baptist Theological Seminary. Riley pastored several other churches in Greenville County besides Washington and Greer First. Records show that he also served White Oak in Greenville, Brushy Creek, Taylors, Fairview and Tigerville.

While Harry Lee Riley was at Washington, the membership increased from 230 to 243. Twelve were baptized, and eight joined the church by letter (Kinard, *A Strong Tower*, pp. 70-71).

REV. W.P. HOLLAND
(1910)

Rev. W.P. Holland served Washington briefly in 1910. He was listed as a delegate to the 1910 meeting of the North Greenville Baptist Association. For that year, the church reported five baptisms, one transfer by letter and a church membership of 242.

> **It wasn't until 1916 that the church would have worship services every Sunday.**

In 1910, church services were held one Sunday a month. Church business meetings would often take place on Saturday afternoons. It was at those meetings that decisions involving the church were made and church discipline was meted out. In the early days, church minutes often speak of those being brought before the body for drunkenness, adultery or other lewd and immoral behavior. The accused would be given the opportunity to publicly repent, at which time they would be restored to fellowship. If they refused to answer the charges or repent, they would be excluded from the body. Even when church services were not being held, Sunday school would be in session four Sundays a month.

It wasn't until 1916 that the church would have worship services

every Sunday. But, for some reason, in 1919 the church reverted back
to just two services a month. It would be 1940 before the church would
again resume services every Sunday.

At the 1911 annual session of the North Greenville Baptist Association,
the group heard an intriguing report from the committee on public morals.

> "We call attention to the evils of smoking. And
> also we would like to call attention to the soft
> drink habit among our people. Many are foolishly
> wasting their means in this unnecessary
> practice, bowing to the feet of another monster
> who will ultimately command you at his will. Use
> of profanity and card playing disapproved."

I wonder what these early guardians of public morals would think if
they could come into the twenty-first century and see where we are today
morally and spiritually.

REV. J. DEAN CRAIN
(1911-1912)

On January 14, 1911, Washington called thirty-year-old Dean Crain to
become their next pastor. A native of the so-called Dark Corner section of
northern Greenville County, Crain was a product of Ebenezer Welcome
Baptist Church, where he and his brother Beauford were baptized on
the same day. Dean and Beauford came from a family of notorious
moonshiners. He was born on October 26, 1881, and graduated from
North Greenville Academy, which was little more than a high school
in those days, and Furman University. Crain was a much-respected
Baptist statesman. He served as president of the South Carolina Baptist

Rev. J. Dean Crain

Convention, held a number of positions in the Southern Baptist Convention, and was, for several years, a trustee of Furman University. He was instrumental in the move of Furman's downtown campus to its current location. Undoubtedly, his greatest years of ministry were at Pendleton Street Baptist Church in Greenville, where he served from 1931 until his retirement in 1952. He died suddenly early in the morning of January 10, 1955, and was widely mourned — not just in the state of South Carolina, but all over the country. In fact, upon his death, Mrs. Dean Crain received a letter from President Dwight Eisenhower, which recalled the time he heard the great pastor pray at the State House in Columbia during one of his visits there. He wrote:

> "As I listened to his prayer on the steps of the Capitol in Columbia, I was so impressed with his earnestness and simplicity that I inquired about him and learned of the high esteem in which he was held throughout the State"
> (Westmoreland, *J. Dean Crain*, pp. 144-145).

Crain's brief time at Washington was notably a time of considerable growth. There were sixty-eight baptisms and thirteen received by letter. Church membership was 290.

Recognizing the need for a school in the community, Mr. S.R. Roe

The old Washington schoolhouse that was demolished in July 1989.

agreed to sell a lot to the Washington District school trustees for $5.00 in August 1914. A frame building was erected for the purpose of housing a grammar school. The building accommodated grades one through seven. A large central room was divided into three sections, with each section being heated by a coal stove. Restrooms were outside the building, and the school water supply came from a nearby well with a hand pump. Later, a separate building was constructed to serve as the lunchroom where meals were served. In later years, Mr. Harold Campbell bought the lunch room building from the church and moved it behind his house for a utility building. It still stands today. The schoolhouse was eventually bricked and served as a public school building until June 1955. The church later bought the building and housed the church kindergarten there for several years. It also served as a church fellowship building for a time and was then eventually demolished. (Information found in church history room from an interview with Joe Henderson).

REV. W.J. BOLT
(1913-1916)

Rev. W.J. Bolt

William Jesse Bolt was born September 29, 1883, in Anderson County, South Carolina. He came to Washington at the beginning of the year in 1913 (Langford, *A Stroll Through* ... , p. 32). As previously mentioned, it was during Bolt's ministry in 1914 that the church began holding services four Sundays a month. Washington was one of only three churches in the North Greenville Association that were doing this.

Under Rev. Bolt's leadership, missions education got its start. In 1914, the YWAs were organized, and then two years later in 1916 the Sunbeam Band, now known as Mission Friends, was begun.

On August 4-5, 1916, the Woman's Missionary Union of the North Greenville Baptist Association met in session at Washington. It was the largest attendance at a WMU meeting in associational history. The minutes of that meeting report, "The hospitality was unsurpassed and the enthusiasm and inspiration received will have a lasting influence on the lives of those present."

It was during Rev. Bolt's ministry at Washington that church membership climbed to over 300, and by the time he left in September 1916, it was up to 336. Forty-six were brought into the church by baptism and forty-seven were received by letter. In September 1916, Pastor W.J. Bolt would conclude his ministry at Washington. He died July 3, 1959, and he and his wife are buried at Woodlawn Cemetery in Greenville.

(Information and picture provided by Mrs. Mary Floyd.)

On April 6, 1917, the United States entered World War I, or, what some would call, "The war to end all wars." More than 2 million Americans fought on the battlefields of France, and when the war would end on November 11, 1918, nearly 117,000 Americans soldiers would be dead. Undoubtedly, there were those from the Washington Church and community who would answer the call to duty and go into battle. Close by was Camp Sevier, an army base where thousands of young men were trained for combat. Area churches, including Washington, would reach out and minister to these soldiers before they made the trip to France.

REV. M.B. BUCKLEY
(1916-1917)

Rev. M.B. Buckley

In December 1916, Washington called M.B. Buckley to become pastor. A native of Missouri, Buckley was ordained to the ministry in 1914 and had, at one time, been associated with the YMCA (Langford, *Pastors of Washington Baptist Church*, p. 9). Little is actually known otherwise about Buckley or his ministry after he left Washington.

REV. ARTHUR L. VAUGHN
(1918-1919)

Rev. Arthur L. Vaughn

Arthur L. Vaughn was pastor of Washington Baptist for about one year. During that time, there was a dramatic decrease in church membership from 336 down to 316. No one joined the church during this time. And still, through the commitment and dedication of God's people, Washington Baptist Church would continue to survive and thrive, always optimistically believing that the best days of the church were yet to come.

—| Chapter Six |—

IN TIMES LIKE THESE
1919-1948

As the year 1919 arrived, the country — and indeed, the world — was still reeling from the effects of the most devastating global war ever fought in history. Weary soldiers returned to their homes and farms. But a transition was quickly taking place in American society. It was a massive transition from a largely agricultural economy to an industrial economy. Perhaps Henry Ford's greatest innovation was not just the automobile, but the way in which it was manufactured. The assembly line was the order of the day, and thousands of jobs were being created in the North. Southerners looking for greater opportunity flocked in large numbers to the automobile factories in Detroit and the tire plants in Akron.

However, the industrial revolution was not just limited to northern factories. Textile mills were springing up across the South in the latter part of the nineteenth century and into the early part of the twentieth century. Eventually, the small town of Greer would boast of being home to four busy cotton mills. People who once worked on small family farms began trading mule-drawn plows for weaving machines. Many still continued to farm while working a shift in town. These cotton mills provided a steady income for a lot of Southerners. Many of these people eventually moved from the farm to textile villages, where their lives revolved around work, worship and leisure activities. Churches, stores and recreational facilities were provided by the textile companies and were often built close to the mill so people could walk from their homes (also provided by the mill) to work and church and shopping. A new way of life had come to America, and days of prosperity lay ahead.

REV. SAMUEL P. COGBURN
(1919-1926)

Rev. Samuel P. Cogburn

In February of 1919, Washington called a new pastor to their church. He was a young, thirty-six-year-old bachelor by the name of Samuel P. Cogburn. During his time at Washington, he boarded with the Bomar family at their home behind the church on Bomar Road.

The late Bernice B. Snyder, a longtime Washington member who was a young girl at the time of Cogburn's ministry, recalled in an essay she wrote during the celebration of the church's 175th anniversary:

"I can remember Rev. S.P. Cogburn. He did his visiting by walking (of course there weren't that many cars at that time). When you saw him you

knew he was coming to eat with you. He didn't
always walk in the road. He would take short cuts
through the woods and fields. If you knew where
I grew up (on West Gap Creek Road) there is a
steep hill behind the house. As he was coming

Centennial celebration, October 30, 1919.

for a visit one afternoon he fell across a terrace.
It didn't bother him. He always carried his Bible
and would read and study while waiting for the
meal to be cooked. He was never married and
boarded with Mr. and Mrs. Jim Bomar."

Cogburn's ministry was noteworthy for a number of reasons. First of all, it was during his tenure that church membership topped 400. Rev. Cogburn baptized 151 people during his seven years at Washington. Evidently, there was a great revival in 1922, because that year he baptized forty. Seventy-two additions came by letter.

It was also while Cogburn was pastor that the church celebrated its centennial. It was quite a celebration and the entire church family gathered on the front steps of the church for a group photograph commemorating the momentous and historical event.

In 1919, the Southern Baptist Convention entered the "$75 Million Campaign" in support of foreign missions.

In 1919, the Southern Baptist Convention entered into what would become known as the "$75 Million Campaign." This drive was intended to support foreign missions. Washington has always had a firm commitment to missions, contributing millions of dollars over the years to the Cooperative Program and through special mission offerings like the Lottie Moon Christmas Offering.

At the thirty-second meeting of the North Greenville Baptist Association held at Holston Creek Baptist Church on August 12-14, 1919, Washington pastor S.P. Cogburn was asked to address the group on the subject of the $75 million campaign. He said, in part, "We are commanded to go into all the world and to make disciples of all nations. We are commanded to teach the whole truth. Jesus bought our salvation with His own precious blood. He paid our greatest debt. And, in His last command, He made us responsible to tell a lost world the plan of salvation. Thus, we owe to the world an honest debt. That debt has never been paid. Over one half of the world is yet in darkness. But the great hour has struck. The call comes today as never before. All doors are open and all the nations are ready to receive the Gospel message of peace and salvation. Those who have long groped in darkness are now calling for the light. Shall we heed the call?" That year Washington Baptist Church contributed $836.70 exclusively for foreign missions.

On August 23, 1923, Washington experienced a great loss with the passing of its first historian, deacon, and longtime church and associational clerk, J. Tupper Henerey. That year, the North Greenville Baptist Association passed a resolution honoring the memory of Henerey, which said:

> "J. Tupper Henerey was born September 25, 1855 at Charleston, South Carolina. He united with the Citadel Square Baptist Church. When just a youth he moved to Greenville County and brought his letter to Washington Baptist Church. He remained a faithful member of this church until he went to his reward August 23, 1923. He was clerk of North Greenville Baptist Association from its organization until his death: a period of thirty-six years. Whereas it has pleased our Heavenly Father to take out of this world the soul of our brother, J. Tupper Henerey, therefore, be it

resolved: first we bow with humble submission
to the will of our Heavenly Father who doeth all
things well, second that we inscribe a page in
our minutes to his memory, third, that a copy of
these resolutions be sent to the bereaved family,
and to *The Baptist Courier* for publication."
(Associational Minutes)

Washington members in the late 1920s to early 1930s. Included are:
(first row, left to right): Richard Howell, Francise Berry, Crandell Howell,
Oris Berry, Don Bruce, Horace Berry, and Dean Bruce.
(second row, left to right): P.L. Bruce, unknown, Shields Hardin,
Elizabeth Bomar, Fannie Berry, SC Berry, B.C. Berry, Annie Berry
holding Martha Berry, Etta Berry, and Claud Berry.
(third row, left to right): Lydia Berry, Homar Howell, Annie Howell,
Mable Howell, unknown, Nora Bruce, Ted Bruce, Broadus Berry,
Lola Barnett, Callie Berry, Alvin Berry, and Tom Bruce.

Another bittersweet moment for the church came in December 1926, when Pastor Cogburn resigned to take another ministerial assignment. Cogburn died in 1973 and is buried in the cemetery of Gowensville First Baptist Church. In 1965, he wrote a letter to Mrs. Peggy Stephens describing his time at Washington:

"Dear Mrs. Stephens,
Early in the year 1919 I became pastor of the
Washington Baptist Church and was pastor for
almost seven years. In 1919 the church was 100
years old. The centennial was observed that year
(1919). During that year 40 members were added
to the church (22 by baptism and 18 by letter).
The Washington Church went over the top in its
pledge to the $75,000,000 Campaign. A little
book, as well as I remember, giving some of the
history of the Washington Church was in the
hands of Brother Tupper Henerey. Brother King,
a former pastor of the Washington Church
may be in a position to give you information.
He had a number of minutes of the
North Greenville Baptist Association.
Yours Sincerely,
S.P. Cogburn
Rt. 2, Landrum, South Carolina"

REV. HENRY CLAYTON HESTER
(1927-1928)

Rev. Henry Clayton Hester

Henry C. Hester served as Washington's pastor a little less than a year — January 20, 1927, to April 1928. Born in Rutherford County, North Carolina, on December 12, 1887, he attended Furman University and the Southern Baptist Theological Seminary (Langford, *A Stroll Through* ... , p. 37).

Information gleaned from associational records indicates there was a Sunday school enrollment of 400 with an average attendance in 1927 of 126. In 1927, we have the first mention of BYPU (Baptist Young People's Union). Forty were officially enrolled that year, and there thirty Sunbeams on roll.

In October of 1929, the growing and robust economy the country had enjoyed during the "Roaring Twenties" came to a screeching halt when the stock market crashed. Soup lines were common sights in the big cities. Rural families perhaps suffered the least because they lived off the land. It wasn't really easy for anyone, though. The people of Washington Baptist Church remained faithful and true to their calling and, as their forefathers had done in lean times, they continued to support and pray for their church.

REV. SHIELDS HARDIN
(1928-1931)

Rev. Shields Hardin

After the brief ministry of Henry C. Hester, the church extended a call to Greer native Shields T. Hardin. Hardin, a graduate of Furman University and the Colgate Seminary, launched his ministry on May 9, 1928.

Hardin's ministry was a time of growth, unity and consolidation. In an effort to make contact with members who had fallen away, the church, in conference on August 4, 1929, sent a letter to each family in Washington notifying them of the church's intention to revise its membership roll. The letter lamented, "The Washington Baptist Church has revised its church roll and finds that twenty-five percent of the members seldom, if ever, come to church." It went on to say, "If you are one of the inactive members, we earnestly beg you to reconsecrate your life to the Master and come help us support the church and its work." The resolution of the church stated its intention to purge the rolls of those who did not, in proper order, re-establish their relationship with the church.

It was in October of 1929 that the church was on the move again, literally. When the church building was originally constructed in 1899 during the ministry of Pastor J.E. McManaway, the front entrance of the church faced the cemetery and the present Bomar Road. With the increase of traffic flow on Highway 14 the decision was made to turn the building so that it would now face Highway 14.

The author remembers Mrs. Bernice Snyder's recollection of how her own father went to the old Camp Sevier in Taylors and procured poles to put under the building so it could be moved with the help of "mule power." It must have been quite a spectacle that day, because those young children who witnessed it still recalled it decades later with a sense of awe and wonder. Also at that time, some Sunday school rooms were added for the growing church.

When Washington was originally built in 1899, the front entrance faced the cemetery and Bomar Road.

In 1929, Washington Church was meeting regularly on the first and fourth Sundays of the month. They observed the Lord's Supper twice that year and baptized twelve. There were just three reported enrolled in BYPU in 1929, and $237 was contributed to the fledgling Cooperative Program.

Baptist historian Joe M. King describes the Cooperative Program as the "great success story of Southern Baptists" (Owens, *Saints of Clay*, p. 126).

Prior to 1925, Southern Baptist churches were bombarded by those soliciting funds for various institutions and causes. Seminaries, colleges, hospitals, orphanages, and a variety of mission organizations would contact pastors and plead for time to come to their churches, speak on behalf of their causes, and then take an offering for support of their causes. After extensive study, the Southern Baptist Convention came up with an ingenious plan — which many believe was an inspired plan. Churches would designate a certain percentage of their total annual income to convention causes and send these monies to the Southern Baptist Convention, where they would be equitably divided among these various ministry needs. Today, Cooperative Program gifts are divided between the Southern Baptist Convention and the state conventions.

Through the years, Washington Baptist Church has strongly believed in and supported the Cooperative Program. It is a bond that keeps our 30 thousand plus churches together. Our churches must be constantly educated and reminded of the great work of the Cooperative Program.

In August 1931, the church bid farewell to Pastor Shields Hardin. Forty-one baptisms were reported during Hardin's three-year tenure at Washington, and he left with the well wishes of the church. Much had been accomplished during his brief ministry at Washington.

REV. L.B. WHITE
(1932-1938)

Rev. L.B. White

When Rev. L.B. White came to be Washington's pastor in January, 1932, the community, and indeed, the nation were still reeling from the effects of the Great Depression. Herbert Hoover was still in the White House and the country was busy trying to figure out how to re-ignite a slumping economy. It was into this backdrop that the fifty-six-year-old Pastor White would come. White, who at one time pastored Holly Springs Baptist Church in Inman, was described by Holly Springs historian Joann Sloan as being "a warm hearted, gracious man who lived the Christian principles that he taught" (Langford, *Pastors of Washington Baptist Church*, p. 10). Could any greater accolade be assigned to a pastor

Above is a "Primary Department Promotion Certificate" given
to Odell Howard in 1933 by Pastor L.B. White and
Mrs. B.C. Berry, Superintendent Primary Department.

than that?

One member of Washington, the late Mrs. Betty H. Mason, who was just a child during White's pastorate, described him as being a man short in stature. She recalled that his feet didn't touch the floor as he sat in the pulpit chair on the platform. She remembered his legs dangling as he sat preparing to preach.

Be that as it may, L.B. White was not short on hard work when it came to fulfilling his ministerial tasks. His years at Washington were years of growth, spiritually as well as numerically. When he arrived on the field, he found a church membership that, at its height, had reached well over 400. When he came to Washington in 1932, it was down to 326. When he left in 1938, it was back up to 369. During his tenure, he baptized forty-nine new additions. In 1933 alone, twenty-eight were baptized. Forty-five joined by letter while he was there. By this time, Washington was having services every Sunday.

At the meeting of the North Greenville Baptist Association in August 1932, Washington's Sunday school superintendent reported a Sunday school enrollment of 289 with an average attendance of 118. For the first time, Sunday school was graded by age, with the enrollment as follows:

Beginners 3-5: 16   Intermeds 13-16: 41
Primaries 6-8: 41   Young People 17-24: 71
Juniors 9-12: 38   Adults 25 and up: 74

These statistics give us a snapshot of Washington's demographic makeup back in the early 1930s. What is especially interesting is the number of young people in the church at that time who were involved in Sunday school. And this, of course, speaks of a growing, vibrant congregation that was flourishing.

In March 1938, the church said goodbye to Rev. L.B. White as he left the grateful congregation with their best wishes. He would live just two years longer, going home to be with the Lord on March 1, 1940.

Between the years 1932-1938, the country was slowly but surely pulling itself out of the pits of the Great Depression. In March, 1933 Franklin Delano Roosevelt would be inaugurated as President of the United States, and he would remind the nation in his inaugural address that "the only thing we have to fear is fear itself." Understanding that drastic times require drastic means, Roosevelt began implementing the measures of what he would call "The New Deal." Public jobs were created by the scores. The Civilian Conservation Corps would be just one of the job-creating programs emerging from the New Deal. Young men were brought into government employment and worked on public projects such as roads, public parks, and other facilities like that. About two miles south of Washington Baptist Church, right off Highway 14, one of these Civilian Conservation Corps camps would be established. A lot of people were stationed in this particular camp, including the son of famed physicist Albert Einstein. In fact, Einstein himself one time visited his son at this camp. To this very day, CCC Camp Road off Highway 14 marks the location of this important landmark that is no longer standing.

> **Famed physicist Albert Einstein's son was stationed at the Civilian Conservation Corps Camp, right off of Highway 14. Einstein one time visited his son there.**

While America was in its slow recovery from the Great Depression, there was a dark specter rising in Germany that would soon make a devastating global impact. Adolf Hitler was rising to political prominence in Germany and the Nazis began their fateful march toward the west. Soon, the peaceful lives of those living in the Washington community would once again be disrupted by a call to arms.

REV. DWIGHT L. BRAGG
(1938-1942)

Upon Rev. L.B. White's departure from Washington in March 1938, the church, once again, found itself in search of a pastor. In June of that year, they called thirty-three-year-old Dwight Bragg to lead the church.

This young, dynamic preacher and his family soon found a home in the hearts of the people. Popular, outspoken and animated in the pulpit,

Rev. Dwight L. Bragg

he led the church very effectively during his four-year ministry at Washington.

Bragg was born September 9, 1905, in Woodruff, South Carolina. He became a Christian at the age of seventeen and was ordained to the ministry by El Bethel Baptist Church in Greer. He was educated at North Greenville College, Furman University, and Southwestern Baptist Theological Seminary in Fort Worth, Texas. Before coming to Washington, Bragg pastored Camp Creek Church from 1934 to 1936, and Locust Hill Church from 1936 to 1938. Dwight Bragg was married to the former Agnes L. Hinton, and they had two children: Malcom and Lottie Jo (Flynn, *History of First Baptist Church of Taylors, S.C.*, p. 54.)

An important milestone was reached during the ministry of Dwight Bragg. He became Washington's first full-time pastor.

At the fifty-first annual meeting of the North Greenville Baptist Association on August 16-17, 1938, delegates from Washington attending the meeting included: J.F. Ballenger, Joe Howell, Harold Hill, G.L. Brown, and G.E. Wilson. At that meeting, Washington reported the value of its property as being $6,000, and the pastor's salary that year was a whopping $493.13! Total contributions to the Cooperative Program were $50.81, with total missions giving coming in at $1,000.75.

When Dwight Bragg became Washington's first full-time pastor, it was determined that a new parsonage should be constructed on property adjacent to the church. Property for the new pastor's home was promptly donated by Mrs. N.E. Bright, with another portion of the lot being given by Mr. and Mrs. J.J. Tapp. Lumber for the project was sawn and stacked on the church property and ready for use. Plans for construction had to be delayed with the outbreak of World War II because building materials were in such short supply (Lancaster, *How Washington Baptist Church Built Its Parsonage*).

Dwight Bragg would faithfully serve the church until 1942, when he left to complete his education at Southwestern Baptist Theological seminary in Fort Worth, Texas. During his four-year ministry at Washington, he would baptize forty-four people, and seventy-one would unite with the church by letter.

Rev. Dwight L. Bragg was Washington's first full-time pastor. In later years, he would become their first pastor emeritus.

In later years, Rev. Bragg would return to Washington in a different role. In the late 1980s, he was elected to be Washington's first pastor emeritus during the ministry of Rev. Jim Ramsey. This honor bestowed upon the aging preacher bespoke the fondness and affection the church held for him. To this day, "Preacher Bragg" is lovingly remembered by those who knew him.

REV. O.B. LANCASTER
(1942-1952)

On May 24, 1942, Washington Baptist Church welcomed thirty-four-year-old O.B. Lancaster as their newest pastor.

Lancaster was born March 1, 1908, in Atlanta, Georgia. As a youth,

Rev. O.B. and Anniebelle Lancaster

he attended schools in Polk County, North Carolina, and Spartanburg County, South Carolina. He graduated from Furman University in 1940, and in 1944 he began studies at the Southern Baptist Theological Seminary in Louisville, Kentucky.

On June 28, 1927, O.B. Lancaster married the former Anniebelle Swain of Gaffney, South Carolina. The couple had two children: Earl Dupre and Martha Jeanette. He served a number of churches in Polk and Rutherford counties, in North Carolina, before coming to Washington in 1942. (Information supplied by Lancaster's grandson, Rev. Keith Lancaster.)

O.B. Lancaster began his work immediately at Washington with his characteristic energy and enthusiasm. Church membership had topped 400 for the first time during the tenure of Dwight Bragg, so the stage had been set for further growth, and the young Lancaster took full advantage of the opportunities set before him. He tirelessly visited the homes, farms, factories and hospitals of the community, and immediately began endearing himself to the people of Greer in general and Washington in particular.

The one dark spot of Lancaster's time at Washington was that — for a portion of it, at least — the nation was embroiled in World War II. Once again, as they had done on every other occasion, the men and women of Washington responded to the call to arms. Members of the church who served in the armed forces during the war included:

E.B. Caldwell

Ray Hill

Lewis Wood

Ralph Lynn

Rufus Hill

Thomas Ponder

Vardry Howard

Dan Ray Jr.

James Ponder

Sam Tapp

Melvin Lynn

Melvin Bailey

Kent Ponder

Bill Gibson

King Paris

Marvin Wilson

Horace Berry

Miller Tapp

Crandell Howell

James Hill

Joe Shockley

Perry Shockley

Jasper Lee Tolbert

Manning Staggs

A.J. Lynn

T.J. Tapp

Carroll Bomar

Marshall Austin

Billy Green

Charles Thompson

Harold Dean Bruce

Martin Tooke Jr.

James Holiday

Harold Campbell

J.D. Lister

Brockman Moon

Preston Bruce Jr.

Hulon Lister

Lauren Seay

Elliott Morrow

Conway Howell

Alvin Ponder

S.J. Harvey

Willie B. Ponder

O'neal Coggins

Though two were wounded in the war (Manning Staggs and Sam Tapp), all of Washington's sons who served returned alive and well (Lancaster, *How Washington Baptist Church Built Its Parsonage*).

Shortly after O.B. Lancaster became pastor of Washington Baptist Church, there was renewed talk of building a parsonage for the minister and his young family. As explained earlier, plans for the house were

Rev. O.B. Lancaster and his deacons, 1945.

actually made in 1940 during the Bragg ministry, but delayed because of the war. Finally, after the war ended in 1945, construction began in earnest. Much of the labor on the parsonage was freely contributed by church members, and on December 11, 1945, the house was completed and occupied by the Lancaster family.

Members of the Building Committee included J.L. Moon, A.D. Turner, and Harold Hill. The memorable motto of this building project was "Let us do all to the glory of God."

The information used here was from the booklet that was written by O.B. Lancaster and published in July 1946, entitled, *How Washington Baptist Church Built Its Parsonage.*

The parsonage was finally sold many years later to Mr. Oran Howard of the Mount Lebanon community

A copy of How Washington Baptist Church Built Its Parsonage *by Rev. O.B. Lancaster, July 1946.*

who had it moved onto his property in 1998, where it still stands and serves as a rental house.

In August 1951, the old "Line School" house and property was purchased by Washington Baptist Church and converted to a mission church/Sunday school. Hulon Arms and others preached and taught there on a weekly basis. Classes were held in the old schoolhouse until 1954. In 1956, the property was sold by sealed bids.

——| Chapter Seven |——
GREEN PASTURES
1949-1974

O.B. Lancaster's ministry at Washington Baptist Church was a building and growth ministry. Not only was the church membership built from 405 when he arrived to 566 when he left the church, but it was also under his leadership that a beautiful parsonage was constructed. And it was during Lancaster's tenure that an educational annex was added onto the back of the church building. Approximately twenty rooms were added, and a new heating system was installed.

At the end of 1952, Rev. O.B. Lancaster announced his resignation and the news was met with great sadness by members of the church. He was leaving to become the pastor of Brandon Baptist Church, located in the Brandon Mill community of Greenville. Lancaster's ministry at Washington was deemed a great success according to anyone's standard. During his ten years, 322 were added to the membership roll — 183 by baptism and 139 by letter.

Rev. Lancaster would remain popular among the Washington family over the years, and was often invited back to speak on special occasions and assist in funeral services up until his death in 1985. Mrs. Lancaster would follow him in death in 1989. They are buried in the cemetery of the First Baptist Church of Green Creek in Green Creek, North Carolina.

REV. E.B. LOWERY
(1953-1955)

Rev. E.B. Lowery

E.B. Lowery was a native of Lancaster, South Carolina, and graduated from Furman University (Langford, *Pastors of WBC*, p. 11). While it's not always easy following a popular and successful pastor in a church, Lowery did a good job early on establishing himself as a caring and compassionate leader and effective pulpiteer.

In the 1953 associational minutes of the North Greenville Baptist Association, the following officers and leaders were listed for Washington Baptist Church:

E.B. Lowery — Pastor
Fred J. Rector — Deacon Chairman
Charles Belue — Choir Director
Lindsey Lynn — Sunday School Director
Darwin Gibson — Training Union Director
Mrs. W.W. Barnett — WMU Director
Fred Rector — Brotherhood Director

Thurmon O. Sudduth — Church Treasurer

Mrs. Paul Barton — Church Clerk

Associational messengers from Washington Baptist Church to the annual meeting held on September 1-2, 1953, at Gowensville and Forestville churches included:

Rev. and Mrs. E.B. Lowery

Mrs. Lindsey Lynn

Mr. and Mrs. Manning Staggs

Mrs. Fred Rector

Harold Hill

Mr. and Mrs. E.F. Tapp

W. Bruce

Bomar Wood

Mr. and Mrs. Paul Barton

News of note for the 1954 church year, according to associational minutes, was the purchase of a new baby grand piano. This piano was used for better than sixty years until the purchase of a new Steinway. It is now in the choir room and still provides good service to the music program of Washington.

Music has always played a prominent role in the life and ministry of Washington Baptist Church. Following the resignation of Charlie Belue as Washington's minister of music, the church called Hugh Atkins to fill the position in 1954. Hugh and his new wife, the former Sara Mason, soon became favorites among the congregation, and he was able to take the music

Sara and Hugh Atkins

ministry to the next level. Hugh served at Washington for a number of years, and later led music at several other area churches, including Brandon, Victor, Double Springs and Pleasant Grove. Later, Hugh and Sara would return to Washington and remain as faithful members of the church. Hugh sang in the choir and Sara became an active leader in the nursery and preschool department, working tirelessly and faithfully until her death in January 2019.

During the Lowery years, the church ordained Leland Browder to the Gospel ministry. This took place on January 19, 1955.

On April 3, 1955, Rev. E.B. Lowery announced his resignation as pastor, effective April 13. During Lowery's tenure, thirty-five were brought into the fellowship by baptism and twenty-three came by letter. The Lowerys left with the well wishes of the Washington family, and Dr. Robert Lamb from North Greenville College was asked to supply the pulpit through the month of May.

The open-air baptistry.

It was in 1955 that the church began renovating the property around the building. Grading was done for some much-needed parking space. The general improvement of the grounds made it necessary to remove the outdoor baptismal pool that had been used for so many years. Baptisms at Washington in the old days were labor-intensive, with water being hauled to the church by wagon or truck from nearby Beaver Dam Creek.

Many happy memories were associated with the old open-air baptistry, but a lot of people were happy to see the baptistry moved indoors.

REV. WILLIAM M. KING
(1955-1959)

Rev. William M. and Doris King

In June 1955, Washington extended a pastoral call to Rev. William M. King. A native of Rock Hill, South Carolina, King was born April 6, 1926. He was a graduate of North Greenville College and Furman University, and did further work at Southeastern and Southwestern seminaries. In 1949, he married Doris Clayton, and they had three children: Tommy, Janice and Clayton.

These were years of continued progress for the church. In 1956, the mission church property on Jordan Road was sold by sealed bids. The money from the sale of this property would provide funds for two important projects that would soon be launched.

Later in 1956, the church agreed to a major renovation of the sanctuary. A new front entrance was constructed and stained glass windows, new pews and carpet were installed.

On January 13, 1957, the $10,000 mortgage the church had taken to pay for these renovations was burned on the front steps of the sanctuary.

In 1957, Washington learned of the school district's intention to sell the old Washington schoolhouse and property across from the church on Highway 14. The congregation voted to purchase the property for use as recreational space, and an offer of $2,000 was submitted. The offer was refused, but a resubmitted offer of $3,000 was finally accepted, and the church acquired the property and the building.

Further building improvements were made in 1958 when the basement of the educational facility was painted and the floors tiled.

On June 14, 1959, after almost exactly four years as pastor, Rev. William King resigned to become pastor of Hamilton Baptist Church in Hamilton, North Carolina. His last day at Washington was July 11, 1959. It was with much regret that the church accepted his resignation. He, Mrs. King and their three children would be greatly missed. Pastor King accomplished much in his brief time at Washington. The church moved forward and made much progress during his tenure, and the people were happy with the direction they were moving in. During Rev. King's time at the church, seventy-five people were added to the rolls by baptism and eighty-seven were accepted by letter.

A NEW ASSOCIATION

Since 1887, Washington Baptist Church had been an active member of the North Greenville Baptist Association. Over the years, as more people began moving into the Greenville/Spartanburg area, more churches were springing up around Greer — especially on the east side in and around Spartanburg County. Several area pastors, including Washington's own W.M. King, began envisioning a new association that would accommodate area churches that were affiliated with the existing Greenville, Spartanburg, and North Greenville associations.

On Wednesday, March 4, 1959, ten pastors met for an "informed discussion" about establishing a new Baptist association. They agreed to meet again on May 6 for another meeting that would include some denominational leaders who could give them more formal guidance and direction.

Determining that they were, indeed, being led by the Lord to move forward, an organizational meeting to form the new Greer Baptist Association was held on July 24, 1959, at Duncan First Baptist Church. At that meeting, the association was officially constituted — and the first annual meeting of the Greer Baptist Association was held in the afternoon and evening of October 27, 1959, at Victor Baptist Church in Greer. At that meeting, twenty-one area churches were present, and all officially became a part of the organization.

On Wednesday, March 4, 1959, ten pastors met for an "informed discussion" about a new Baptist association.

The Greer Baptist Association thrived for fifty-four years until it was dissolved in 2013, when the Three Rivers Baptist Association was formed from the union of the North Greenville and Greer associations.

In its fifty-four-year existence, the Greer Baptist Association had only four directors of missions, each of whom served with distinction:

Rev. Wyatt Garrett
Rev. Jimmy Skinner

Dr. Cleatus Blackmon
Rev. Tom Capps

(Information on the organization of the Greer Baptist Association came from *The Minutes of the First Annual Session of the Greer Baptist Association, 1959.*)

REV. KENNETH M. NEWTON
(1959-1972)

Rev. Kenneth M. Newton

Following the resignation of W.M. King, the church called upon Rev. Leon Latimer to be their interim pastor for a time. He served from July 5, 1959, until January 1, 1960. On November 22, 1959, the church called Rev. Kenneth Newton of Baltimore, Maryland, to be their next pastor. He was, however, unable to move to South Carolina until the following January. Consequently, his first Sunday at Washington was January 3, 1960.

A South Carolina native, following military service and ministerial education, Newton pastored for a time in Baltimore before his call to Washington. Newton, his wife, DeAlva, and two sons, Steve and Phil, would move to the community, and two more children would later be added to the family — Ann and Frank.

Rev. Newton soon endeared himself to church members with his personable manner, quick wit, strong biblical preaching, and loving pastoral care. His uncanny ability to show up at members' homes around mealtime is remembered to this very day. He enjoyed visiting homes, hospitals and nursing homes. He fished and hunted rabbits with the men of the church and established relationships in the Greer community that remained strong for years to come. This writer had the honor of calling him friend, and I will always remember his reply when I told him I appreciated him. He would quickly answer, "I appreciate being appreciated!"

In January 1961, the church once again became debt-free after paying off the new air-conditioning system that had been installed in the church and educational facility. With the future in view, on February 19, 1961, a committee was formed to investigate the possibility of constructing a much-needed new sanctuary. Architect Maurice Johnson of Spartanburg was commissioned to draw up plans for the new facility. Yeargin Construction company of Greenville was contracted for the construction, and the church borrowed $150,000 from Greer Federal to pay for the project. With all the details worked out, ground was broken for the new sanctuary in April 1964.

Construction of the Washington steeple, 1964.

The church entered into their new building on November 22, 1964, and the first person baptized in the new baptistry was Mrs. Lillian Bruce on November 29, 1964. The first couple married in the new church was Mr. and Mrs. Doyle Wilson.

Reflecting on the construction of the beautiful modern and spacious sanctuary, one marvels at the faith and vision of Washington's leaders and members when the idea of the new building was first conceived in 1961. Washington was still, at that time, largely a rural church. The community had experienced little growth in decades, and yet the people had the faith and vision to build a building that is still accommodating the congregation and community nearly sixty years later. While there have been renovations and improvements over the years, it still remains a building that the members of Washington can certainly be proud of. In 1967, there was a recommendation that the church begin a kindergarten program. Mrs. Paul Barton was chosen to be its director, and the program launched in the fall of 1968.

The kindergarten of Washington continued for several years, educating and introducing the Gospel of Christ to a whole generation of children, many of whom still attend the church and hold prominent positions of leadership in the church.

Geneva Barton and her kindergarten class.

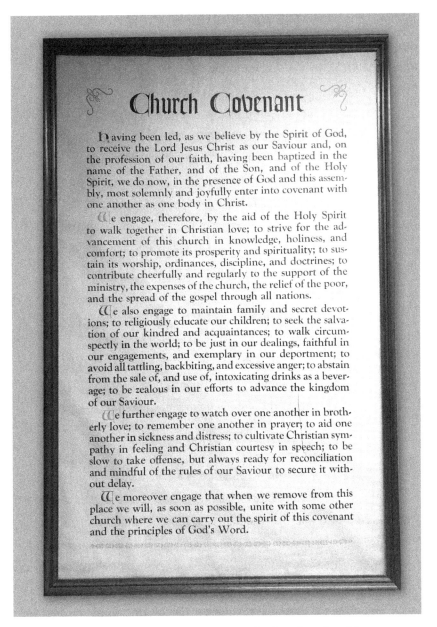

Church Covenant

Having been led, as we believe by the Spirit of God, to receive the Lord Jesus Christ as our Saviour and, on the profession of our faith, having been baptized in the name of the Father, and of the Son, and of the Holy Spirit, we do now, in the presence of God and this assembly, most solemnly and joyfully enter into covenant with one another as one body in Christ.

We engage, therefore, by the aid of the Holy Spirit to walk together in Christian love; to strive for the advancement of this church in knowledge, holiness, and comfort; to promote its prosperity and spirituality; to sustain its worship, ordinances, discipline, and doctrines; to contribute cheerfully and regularly to the support of the ministry, the expenses of the church, the relief of the poor, and the spread of the gospel through all nations.

We also engage to maintain family and secret devotions; to religiously educate our children; to seek the salvation of our kindred and acquaintances; to walk circumspectly in the world; to be just in our dealings, faithful in our engagements, and exemplary in our deportment; to avoid all tattling, backbiting, and excessive anger; to abstain from the sale of, and use of, intoxicating drinks as a beverage; to be zealous in our efforts to advance the kingdom of our Saviour.

We further engage to watch over one another in brotherly love; to remember one another in prayer; to aid one another in sickness and distress; to cultivate Christian sympathy in feeling and Christian courtesy in speech; to be slow to take offense, but always ready for reconciliation and mindful of the rules of our Saviour to secure it without delay.

We moreover engage that when we remove from this place we will, as soon as possible, unite with some other church where we can carry out the spirit of this covenant and the principles of God's Word.

It's believed that the church covenant was displayed in the old sanctuary until the late 1960s when it was remodeled. The covenant continued to be displayed in the vestibule until the building was demolished in 2007.

THE WASHINGTON WINDOW

In a publication from February 28, 1960, simply entitled, *Washington Baptist Church News*, it was announced:

"In the future we plan to have a church newspaper concerning the events that will take place in our church and other churches pertaining to us. We would like to have people choose a name for this newspaper. Anyone who would like to participate in this, please put your name and the name you would like to enter in our little contest on paper and give it to the pastor. There will be a committee to choose the name to be used. This name and your name will be mentioned in the next issue of the news. Also, we would like for you to turn in any births, deaths, weddings, new homes, military service, or important events and meetings of interest to our church."

The first edition of *The Washington Window* was published on March 27, 1960, and in that publication it was announced that Sammy Bomar won the contest of naming the paper and his submission, of course, was *The Washington Window*. From that day on, *The Washington Window* has been continuously published. At first, it appeared monthly, but now it is a weekly publication — mailed to all church members, but also available online for those who request it. Today, the church newsletter is strictly a news and information source.

In addition to news, *The Washington Window* would also print special interest relating to the people of Washington. For example, the October

18, 1964, edition carried this piece about a family in the church who survived the explosion of a hot water heater in their home, something the older members of the church still remember to this day:

> "Did you know that the Mostellers have entered the 'space race' competition against tough odds? The launching pad (their home) was completely destroyed. The hot water heater (rocket) landed in the field 320 feet from their home. We're grateful to God for their safety."

The weekly "Did You Know?" column was a popular feature of *The Washington Window*. Some of the items of special interest from the September 11, 1960. edition included:

> "Did you know ... that Billy Staggs has a new 'go cart?' ... That Mr. and Mrs. L.A. Lynn camped out in the mountains last week? ... That lightning struck the home of Mr. and Mrs. Riley Ray? ... That seventeen men went deep sea fishing?"

Over the years, *The Washington Window* has changed, but people still glean church news and information from its pages, in print and online.

A special day was observed in October 1969, as the church celebrated its 150th anniversary. A pictorial directory was produced, and in the front of that directory were four pages of church history, including Henerey's early history and an additional history leading up to 1969. The anniversary was observed on October 26, 1969, with great celebration and fanfare. Former pastor Rev. Shields T. Hardin spoke on the special occasion, and many church members dressed in period and old-fashioned costumes. A "dinner on the grounds" highlighted the day. Commenting on the momentous occasion, Pastor Newton wrote:

"Ours is a great heritage; for 150 years we have ministered in the name of Christ. Great preachers have preached the 'unsearchable riches of Christ' while loyal, dedicated laymen have led the church from victory to victory.

Our church is rich — not necessarily in buildings or collections, but there is a wealth of faithful members who love Jesus with all their hearts. Our mission is to make Jesus known and to say as Paul, 'God forbid that I should glory

In October 1969, Washington celebrated its 150th anniversary.
Pictured are members in period costumes from that era.

except in the cross of Jesus.' Who knows but that
God has placed us here for such a time as this.
May God bless us as fishers of men as we launch
out into the deep of the Space Age.
Lovingly Yours,
K.N. Newton, pastor"
(from the 1969 church directory)

It was a sad day indeed on April 30, 1972, when Rev. Kenneth Newton announced his resignation as pastor of Washington Baptist Church after nearly thirteen years of faithful service. He would next move to Orangeburg to minister. Newton's tenure at Washington was marked by great progress and growth. The people embraced his vision, and blessing resulted.

During Rev. Newton's years at Washington, 232 members were added to the church by baptism and 478 came by transfer of letter.

The Newtons remained popular in the church, returning

*Mrs. Laura Durham
and Mrs. Geneva Barton
at Washington's 150th
anniversary celebration.*

often for funerals, weddings, and other special occasions. They eventually moved back to the Washington community after retirement, much to the delight of their many friends. In 2004, Rev. Kenneth Newton became Washington's second pastor emeritus and was a regular and faithful church member until his death on October 12, 2011. Mrs. Newton had preceded him in death in July 1996, and both are buried in the Washington cemetery.

Washington's affection for the Newtons was perhaps best expressed by a piece that appeared in the church newsletter shortly before their departure:

"As Brother and Mrs. Newton and family leave
after being with us for twelve and one half years,
and becoming so endeared to all of us,
the words of a poet express our feelings
toward them most appropriately:

'People come into our lives
And walk with us a mile
And then because of circumstance
They only stay awhile.
They serve a need within the days
That move so quickly by,
And then are gone beyond our reach
We often wonder why.
God only knows the reason that
We meet and share a smile —
Why people come into our lives
And walk with us a mile.'"

REV. JOHN B. COMPTON
(1972-1977)

Rev. John B. Compton

On August 27, 1972, Washington Baptist Church voted unanimously to call Rev. John B. Compton as their new pastor.

Originally from Oconee County, South Carolina, Compton was a graduate of Presbyterian College and Southeastern Baptist Theological Seminary in Wake Forest, North Carolina. He, his wife, Anne, and their four daughters — Rachel, Sharon, Jeanie and Christy — came to Washington from Fourth Street Baptist Church in Hartsville, South Carolina.

On December 28, 1975, Washington was blessed to "burn" the mortgage on their sanctuary. Pictured are (left to right): Thurman Sudduth, Darwin Gibson, Lindsey Lynn, Jimmy Barnett, Dan Ray, and Rev. John Compton.

Rev. Compton's first Sunday was also the first Sunday of the new church year, October 1. He and his family were greeted by a large, enthusiastic congregation, and the Lord's Supper was observed on that first Sunday. The new minister was energetic and dedicated to his calling and his new church, and the people were eager to follow his leadership.

STAFF ADDITIONS:
BILL LEE
(Part-Time Minister of Music)

Bill Lee

In September 1971, the church had called Bill Lee, of Greer, to become their new part-time minister of music.

Lee served the church faithfully until his departure in 1977. It was during his tenure at Washington, and during the pastorate of John Compton, that the Washington choir presented the musical "Alleluia," which was based on the music of Bill and Gloria Gaither. During the latter part of 1974 and early 1975, the choir performed this music on several occasions and in different venues. In January 1975, for example, the choir traveled to Homer, Georgia, to present the musical. According to the January 30, 1975, edition of *The Washington Window*, "Decisions for Christ were made in Homer, Georgia, this past Saturday night — and that is what 'Alleluia' is all about!"

So memorable was this performance that the 200th anniversary

6-The Greer Citizen, Greer, S. C., Wed., Sept. 10, 1975

Washington Baptist Church Choir Will Sing In Atlanta

A newspaper clipping from The Greer Citizen, Wednesday, September 10, 1975, about the Washington choir presenting "Alleluia" in Atlanta.

committee decided to reprise "Alleluia" as a part of the church's anniversary celebration on April 7, 2019.

ALAN COCHRAN
(Summer Youth Worker)

In April 1972, Washington extended an invitation to Alan Cochran to become their summer youth worker. Cochran, a student at Furman, was well-liked and performed his duties effectively. He continued to serve the church during the summer for a few years after that. Cochran went on to become a prominent attorney in Greenville until his untimely death to cancer in 2018.

In 1973, two notable events took place at Washington. First, in June of that year, the church purchased a sixty-passenger bus for $7,000. During the early '70s, many churches entered into the bus ministry, transporting

Alan Cochran

people (especially children) to church services. In September 1973, the Durham Educational Scholarship Fund was established by Mrs. Mildred Bruce and Mrs. Minnie Jane Burnett, in memory of Mr. and Mrs. Henry Otis Durham. This fund was intended to assist Washington members with educational expenses. It still exists to this day and has, over the years, helped many young people in their quest for higher education.

——┤ Chapter Eight ├——
A NEW MILLENNIUM
1975-2000

It was during the ministry of John Compton that the church was able to pay off its indebtedness for the construction of the church sanctuary. The mortgage was officially retired in November 1975, and the event was celebrated with a formal mortgage-burning on December 28, 1975. The mortgage was paid off four years ahead of schedule.

A new staff position was established in January 1975, with the calling of John Brown as minister of education and activities. The continued growth of the church and the pastor's emphasis on discipleship and Christian education triggered the bold decision to add another staff member. The church moved a mobile home to the vacant land across Highway 14 for the new minister to live in. Brown served in this position until his resignation in August of 1976.

From 1977 to 1979, Tim Stack served as Washington's youth and children's director. A native of Greer and the son of the late Johnny and Mary Evelyn Stack, Tim coordinated all children and youth activities during the two summers he served. Tim later graduated from Erskine

College and the University of South Carolina School of Law. He married Ann Moore, who was a member of Washington and has deep family roots in the church. They are the parents of one son, John. Tim currently serves as a trustee for the U.S. Department of Justice in Columbia, where he, Ann and John make their home.

The cultural landscape of America was changing drastically in the early and mid-'70s. The Vietnam War was coming to a close, but protests in cities and on college campuses continued. The civil rights movement had expanded to include equal rights for women, and more and more young people were questioning their faith and values. This became a real challenge for the church. However, there were some bright spots, though. A young Josh McDowell — a bright, new Christian apologist — was becoming a popular speaker among young people. His 1972 book, *Evidence That Demands a Verdict*, was a landmark book in the area of Christian apologetics. In the early '70s, "Jesus freaks" made their first appearance. These were, for the most part, young people who found that Christ could make a real difference in their lives. Many had turned from drugs, alcohol, and other illicit activities to faith in Christ. Even though their approach was somewhat unorthodox, they still made a huge impact on their culture. In California, Chuck Smith was baptizing scores of people in the Pacific Ocean. It was there that the first Calvary Chapel was established, a church and a system that has spread across the country.

With all this cultural and societal change, mainline churches and

> **With all the cultural and societal changes of the '70s, Washington was meeting the challenge, with new ways to impact the community for the Lord.**

denomination had a choice: They could either choose to build a wall between themselves and the world, or learn to adapt and try to reach their society with the message of Christ. Washington was meeting the challenge, creating new ways to impact their community for the Lord.

On December 11, 1977, the church was saddened to hear the news that Rev. John Compton was leaving to become pastor of Westminster Baptist Church in Westminster, South Carolina, effective January 1, 1978. He would pastor in Westminster until his retirement in 1996.

Compton's accomplishments were many during his stay at Washington. There were 239 new additions to the church while he was pastor: sixty-three by baptism and 176 by letter. Rev. and Mrs. Compton, at this writing, live in Seneca, South Carolina, and he is the oldest living former pastor of the church.

REV. WILLIAM CASHION
(1978-1985)

Rev. William Cashion

On June 18, 1978, Washington Baptist Church invited Rev. William Cashion to become their thirty-seventh pastor. The thirty-year-old preacher and his wife, Kathy (the former Kathryn Stroud), and two daughters Amy and Melissa, moved into the newly renovated and updated Washington parsonage. After graduating from the Baptist College of Charleston in 1971, Cashion went on to obtain a

Groundbreaking for the new building, November 6, 1978. Pictured are (left to right): Rev. Bill Cashion, Darwin Gibson, and Don Black.

Master of Divinity degree from Southeastern Baptist Theological Seminary in Wake Forest, North Carolina. At the time he was called to Washington, he was pastor of Carolina Pines Baptist Church in Raleigh, North Carolina.

The young, energetic pastor, known to all as "Billy," hit the ground running. The people quickly discovered that their new pastor had a heart for God, His Word and God's people.

Cashion, a former baseball player, saw sports and activities as a means of reaching people for Christ, especially the young people. It was upon his suggestion and vision that the church launched into one of its most ambitious building projects to date: a family life center with an educational wing.

On October 15, 1978, the church agreed to implement the "Together We Build" model for fundraising for the new facility. Then, on April 8, 1979, a "Together We Build" banquet was hosted by the church in the cafeteria of the Greer Middle School. Sixty families pledged their prayer and financial support for the new recreational center. All the busy planning, praying, and pledging resulted in the groundbreaking

Above is the mission team that traveled to Wasilla, Alaska, in 1979.

for the new building on November 6, 1978. M.L. Garrett Construction Company of Greenville was commissioned to do the construction at an estimated cost of $500,000. It was a day of celebration on January 11, 1981, when the church dedicated the new family life center/educational wing. The pastor wrote in program for that day:

"Our goal must always be to glorify the name of our God through the winning of souls to Jesus Christ and adorning those new 'stones' with all the graces of the gospel as we live and teach the truths of God's Holy Word. To this end we dedicate our Family Life Center and Education Wing. 'Unto Him be glory in the church by Christ Jesus throughout all ages, world without end. Amen.' (Ephesians 3:21)."

Outreach and discipleship were very important components of Cashion's ministry at Washington. Evangelism Explosion and Continued Witness Training were two essential teaching tools for soul-winning, and both were implemented at Washington during this time, with teams going out weekly into the community to share their faith.

Once people were won to faith in Christ, they underwent new member training through the use of the *Survival Kit for New Christians*. Here, they learned more about their newfound faith and discovered the importance of daily spiritual growth. For people who had been Christians for a longer period of time, MasterLife groups were begun.

During his years at Washington, Rev. Cashion reached out to the Greenville Braves minor league baseball team, becoming their team chaplain. As a result, several of the team members and their families began attending the church.

Cashion's burgeoning interest in missions also became more and more evident over time. The church started hosting volunteer mission training workshops sponsored by the International Mission Board, and it wasn't long until mission trips within the church were being organized. Pastor Cashion led two mission trips to Ecuador and one to Chile. In addition to these excursions outside of the country, groups were led also to participate in North American mission trips to as far away as Alaska, Michigan and Pennsylvania. Much closer to home, the church participated in mission projects in South Carolina as well.

Many were sad, but not many were surprised when, on May 19, 1985, Rev. Bill Cashion announced his resignation as pastor of Washington Baptist Church to become a missionary to Venezuela. Billy and Kathy Cashion were solidly committed to go into all the world with the good news of Jesus Christ. So along with their two daughters (youngest daughter Katie would come along later) they packed their belongings and entered mission language training school before going on to their destination of Venezuela. They left with the prayers and well wishes of their Washington family. The Cashion family would remain in Venezuela until 1996.

In 1997, Cashion would receive the Doctor of Ministry degree from Mid-America Theological Seminary in Memphis, Tennessee. He served in other key roles with the International Mission Board before returning to the pastorate in 2004 at Bethlehem Baptist Church in Clarksville, Georgia. At this writing, he is professor of missions and evangelism at the T. Walter Brashier Graduate School of North Greenville University. He and Kathy live in Greer and he has numerous opportunities to preach in area churches.

Rev. William Cashion's time at Washington would be remembered as a time of spiritual as well as numerical growth. During his nearly seven-year tenure, he would baptize 180 and see 130 other additions by letter and by statement. His emphasis on missions by going as well as giving is still felt to this day within the church. The Cashion years were important years for Washington Baptist Church.

NICK MORGAN
(Minister of Education and Family Life)

In October 1980, the church invited Mr. Nick Morgan to become their new minister of education and family life. This newly created position filled a real need. Not only did it address the educational and discipleship requirements of the church, but it also enhanced the utilization of the new family life center by emphasizing and developing family and recreational activities.

A native of Atlanta, Georgia, Nick Morgan graduated from Georgia Tech. He served for some time on the staff of Campus Crusade for Christ and received the additional academic degrees of Master of Divinity and

Nick Morgan

Master of Religious Education from Southwestern Baptist Theological Seminary in Fort Worth, Texas.

Nick and his wife, Bonnie, married in 1974. Bonnie was a teacher in public schools for many years and has always been a supporter of and partner in Nick's ministry. In 1988, they welcomed their daughter, Andrea, into their lives, and their family was complete.

During Morgan's eleven-year ministry at Washington Baptist Church, he worked hard to grow the Sunday school by emphasizing outreach and teacher training. He was a big proponent of discipleship training, and the church saw dramatic increases in attendance on Sunday evenings as a variety of different discipleship curricula was offered. He also filled other important roles in the church as the necessity arose. There were times, for example, when he was involved in youth ministry. And during the lengthy interim between Bill Cashion's departure and Jim Ramsey's arrival, Nick Morgan took on much of the pastoral work of counseling and visitation. His tenure at Washington was highlighted by faithful service, and to this day, the people remember him and his family with great fondness and affection.

Morgan resigned in November 1991, after eleven years of dedicated service. He would soon assume a similar position at Northwood Baptist Church in the Charleston association, where he would remain until his retirement after twenty-five years of dedicated ministry.

REV. JIM RAMSEY
(1987-1996)

Rev. Jim Ramsey

On February 1, 1987, after nearly two years without a pastor, Washington Baptist Church unanimously called Rev. Jim Ramsey to be their next minister.

A native of Rock Hill, South Carolina, Ramsey was a graduate of the Baptist College of Charleston and Southeastern Baptist Theological Seminary in Wake Forest, North Carolina. He and his wife, Donya, had one child, Emily, when they arrived at Washington. Their other daughter, Jessica, was born shortly after they came.

The young pastor (he was twenty-nine when he came to Washington) made an immediate impact with his wit, charm and spontaneity. He was noted for his insightful, biblical preaching. The young family was especially popular with the young people of the church, and several young families came into the church family during the Ramsey years.

One of the first acts of the church after Ramsey's arrival was to acknowledge the appreciation the congregation had for Rev. Dwight Bragg's lengthy and effective interim ministry between Cashion and Ramsey. This was a critical period of transformation.

Dwight Bragg had a long and rich history with Washington. He was the church's first full-time pastor, serving between the years 1938 and 1942. "Preacher Bragg," as he was affectionately known, was honored by the church on March 29, 1987, by being named its very first pastor emeritus. On this special day, a portrait of Bragg was presented to the church, and it hung in the vestibule for years. It is now in the History Room.

Dwight Bragg remained a faithful member of Washington until his passing on March 14, 1994.

In the summer of 1989, the decision was made to demolish the old Washington schoolhouse which had stood on the church's property across Highway 14 since 1914. This, of course, was no easy decision, because there were so many tender memories attached to the old school. In the first place, it had served the community well for several years as a place of learning. And then after the building was purchased by the church in 1958, it became a kindergarten facility as well as a recreational area for the church. But due largely to neglect in later years, the building became dilapidated and deemed unsafe for occupancy. Finally, it was brought down in July of 1989. There are still those who remember the schoolhouse with great fondness.

In 1994, Washington Baptist Church celebrated its 175th anniversary. The motto for this yearlong observance was, "In business with God since

Rev. Dwight Bragg (left) being honored as pastor emeritus.
Also pictured is Rev. Jim Ramsey.

Former pastors who attended Washington's 175th anniversary (left to right): Rev. John Compton, Rev. Billy Cashion, Rev. Elton Lane (a minister who was ordained by Washington), Rev. Kenneth Newton, and Rev. Jim Ramsey.

1819." The event was officially commemorated on October 30, 1994. That Sunday morning, the pastor, along with the 175th anniversary committee, were taken to the church by horse and buggy. Many that day donned period costumes to honor the special occasion, and former pastors and church members returned to mark the landmark event. A big meal was served in the family life center for all who attended.

The gradual growth of the church made it necessary to bring permanent clerical and secretarial help to the staff.

Mrs. Peggy Stephens was among the first of these administrative assistants at Washington.

PEGGY STEPHENS
(Administrative Assistant)

A native of Florida, Mrs. Stephens, and her husband, J.C., moved to the area for work-related reasons. The family settled in the Washington

Peggy Stephens

community and soon became an active part of the church family. In the early 1960s, Peggy joined the staff and was largely responsible for editing and publishing the earliest editions of *The Washington Window*. She also took a very active part in the church, leading in mission organizations and faithfully teaching a ladies Sunday school class for many years. Peggy was also the church's financial secretary, and people still fondly remember how, in some lean financial times, her paycheck would often be the last check written — and sometimes she wrote herself no paycheck at all. She was a humble and unselfish servant of God and her passing in 2014 left a great void in the church. In 1989, during the ministry of Rev. Jim Ramsey, Mrs. Gayle Knight became Washington's secretary.

Gale Knight

GALE KNIGHT
(Administrative Assistant)

Gale had been a lifelong member of Washington, except for a period of time when she and her husband, Ronnie, and family attended Northwood Baptist Church. Gale served Washington faithfully for many years until her retirement in March 2001. It wasn't long after her retirement that she and Ronnie returned to Washington as members and have since become actively involved in the life of the church. Ronnie currently serves in many roles, including deacon, church trustee and chairman of the cemetery committee. He also has served on the 200th anniversary committee.

Other staff additions of note include the calling of Karla Ross as minister of music.

KARLA ROSS
(Minister of Music)

Karla Ross

In 1993, after the resignation of then minister of music Stan Jones, Karla Ross was asked to assume the position of interim minister of music until a replacement for Jones could be found. With no prior experience and with some persuasion, she agreed to serve in the interim.

Born into the Washington Church family, Karla is the daughter of Carolyn Ross and the late Joe Ross. Carolyn, on many different occasions, has served as a musician for the church, as well as organist. Karla graduated from Greer High School and entered Carson-Newman University with the intention of studying music. She was already an accomplished vocalist when she entered college, but she soon decided that music was not the direction she wanted to take. She changed her major to physical education, and upon graduation began teaching in public school.

She agreed to serve as a part-time interim minister of music, and was soon asked to fill the position on a permanent basis. She has served faithfully in this role for twenty-six years and counting, and continues to be a blessing to the music ministry of the church.

In 1992, Robin Carlisle was asked to serve as part-time minister of youth.

ROBIN CARLISLE
(Minister of Youth)

Robin Carlisle

Robin had earlier married Tracie Seay, the daughter of Owen Dean and Christine Seay and a lifelong member of Washington. A former member of Tucapau Baptist Church in Wellford, Robin soon became actively involved in the life of Washington Baptist Church, serving as a Sunday school teacher for many years and also as a deacon. Robin had a great love for the youth of the church. In 1992, he was invited to become the church's minister of youth on a part-time basis. He served faithfully in that capacity for about thirteen years, until his resignation in 2005. Robin was noted for his ability to connect with young people on their level. He developed many lasting relationships with those in his youth group, and many of those relationships are still very meaningful to this day.

In 1996, Rev. Jim Ramsey announced his resignation as pastor of Washington. During Ramsey's time at Washington, there were 313 additions to the church — sixty-eight by baptism and 117 by letter. The Ramseys moved to Rock Hill, South Carolina, where he would later tragically die from the effects of a brain tumor.

After the Ramseys' departure, the church called upon former pastor Kenneth Newton to serve as interim pastor. Rev. Newton served well during this difficult transition period. An interim pastor has a unique opportunity to assist a pastor-less church in a number of ways. First, the congregation needs continuity of sound biblical preaching and teaching. This is an ongoing necessity for every church. The interim should encourage, exhort and promote unity among the church family. Sometimes, especially when pastors leave a church under less-than-desirable circumstances, there is a lack of unity and harmony. A good interim pastor can bring people back together and help to pave the way for the next man of God who is called to that congregation. Over the years, Washington has been blessed in this regard — and this is part of the reason that the church has remained strong and united through the years.

Rev. Ron Bryan

REV. RON BRYAN
(1997-1999)

In the early months of 1997, the church unanimously called Rev. Ron Bryan to be their next pastor. A native of North Carolina, he was a graduate of Mars Hill College and Southeastern Baptist Theological Seminary, and would later receive his PhD degree from

Rev. Ron Bryan ascending to the roof of the church to preach, after meeting the church goal of 300 in Sunday school on February 14, 1999.

Glendale University. Bryan spent a majority of his ministry pastoring churches in the eastern part of North Carolina. He and his wife, Barbara, are the parents of two daughters. The Bryans moved to Washington and began establishing relationships with several young couples already in the church, and some who later came into the fellowship. Mentoring and discipling young families, they believed, would be key in the future growth of the church.

Bryan also saw the importance of Sunday school in the life of the church and worked with then director Mike Sweet to promote the growth of the Sunday school. The pastor challenged the church to reach a goal of 300 in attendance in Sunday school, and set the date of Sunday, February 14, 1999, to be high attendance day. As an added incentive, Pastor Bryan agreed to preach from the roof of the church if the goal of 300 was reached. February 14 arrived, and the goal was met and surpassed — so, true to his word, Bryan ascended to the top of the church in an automatic lift, or "cherry picker" as some call it, and preached his sermon. *The Greer*

Citizen, reporting on the event, wrote:

"The Word From Above:
Rev. Ron Bryan, pastor of Washington Baptist
Church, recently fulfilled a promise by climbing
into a bucket truck to preach. Rev. Bryan had
promised to preach from the roof if there were
300 worshipers in attendance in Sunday school
on February 14, and the congregation
met the challenge."

It was also during the year of 1999 that the sanctuary of Washington received a major "face lift." There had been very few physical improvements in the sanctuary since its construction in 1964. The carpet was worn and the design somewhat dated. A major financial gift from the estate of Clara Waters enabled the church to make some big improvements. Along the way, other gifts were given in memory of loved ones to help support the renovation. New paint, and new carpet, as well as some new fixtures, added to the beauty of the auditorium, and painted paneling brightened up the interior considerably. In addition, the baptistry window was enlarged, and a beautiful aluminum cross was on display from the back of the baptistry.

The members of Washington took great pride in the appearance of the church's auditorium. After worshiping in the family life center for the duration of the renovation, they were ready to return to their beautiful new house of worship.

In December 1999, the church bid farewell to the Bryans as they were led to Columbia, where Pastor Bryan would become pastor of Crescent Hill Baptist Church until his retirement. During the Bryan pastorate, the church welcomed a total of 150 additions to the congregation. There

In 1999, Washington saw significant improvements to the sanctuary.

were thirty-two baptisms and fifty-nine other additions by letter or by statement. Also in 1999, Tim Landreth became part-time youth director. Tim is remembered as being a strong Christian role model for the youth. He and his wife, Allison, served faithfully for two years. They, along with their two sons, live in Greenville, South Carolina, where Tim is employed with Prisma Healthcare.

After the Bryans' departure, Washington called on the Rev. Donel Kelley to become their interim pastor.

REV. DONEL KELLEY
(Interim Pastor 2000-2001)

A native of Raleigh, North Carolina, Rev. Kelley had finished his education at North Carolina State University before his call to ministry. After the Lord led him away from the business sector, he enrolled in studies at New Orleans Baptist Theological Seminary in New Orleans, Louisiana. He and his wife, Caroline, ministered in a number of churches in North and South Carolina before coming to Abner Creek Baptist Church in Greer

Rev. Donel Kelley

in 1977. Rev. Kelley remained at Abner Creek for twenty years until his retirement in 1997. Retirement was short-lived for the Kelleys. His reputation as a caring, compassionate pastor and strong Bible preacher made him especially attractive to churches seeking an interim pastor. He served at Pelham First Baptist Church not long after his departure from Abner Creek. He and his wife would later become members of Pleasant Grove Baptist Church in Greer, where he would soon serve effectively as minister to senior adults.

In January 2000, as the new millennium began, the Kelleys started their ministry at Washington. Rev. Kelley quickly endeared himself to the Washington family through his strong teaching and preaching ministry, as well as his warm, personal pastoral skills. Not simply content to come preach three times a week, the new interim pastor visited throughout the community, ministering to those in need and witnessing to the lost. His ministry was a healing time as well. During his eighteen months at Washington, Kelley made a positive impact.

It was during this time that the church became closely associated with the Chosen Children's ministry in Managua, Nicaragua. During the summer of 2000, a mission trip to the Chosen Children's orphanage and children's home was organized. A number of Washington's members, along with members of other churches, traveled to Managua for a life-changing experience. For two of Washington's members in particular, life would never be the same. It was during this time that Kerry and Neltia Henderson began feeling the call of God to international missions. They made their commitment public, and the church pledged to pray for them and support them in their decision in any way possible. The church would continue a relationship with Chosen Children for some time after that, and later would expand their reach in Nicaragua even further.

Through visiting, ministering and witnessing, Kelley made a positive impact during his eighteen months at Washington.

As 2000 came to a close, the church found itself stronger and more united than ever — thanks in large part to the prayers and support of the committed members of Washington, as well as the effective leadership of Pastor Kelley.

Don and Caroline Kelley would later join Washington Baptist Church, where they would become beloved members. Unfortunately, not long after they returned to Washington, Caroline fell victim to cancer and went to be with the Lord in September 2012. Later, Rev. Kelley would marry Ruth Lister Tooley, and at this writing, both are very active members of Washington. Don has taught a senior adult couple's Sunday school class for a number of years, and it is one of the strongest, fastest-growing classes in the church.

──────┤ Chapter Nine ├──────
FORWARD BY FAITH
2001-2019

The new century and new millennium arrived with much fanfare and expectation. Prophets of doom predicted a major catastrophe as sophisticated computer systems tried to make the change from the 1900s to the 2000s. The so-called "Y2K scare" struck terror in the hearts of many, but fortunately the new century arrived with little if any problem.

Meanwhile, the good people of Washington Baptist were still adjusting to life without a full-time pastor to lead them. The church was truly blessed to have secured the services of transitional pastor Rev. Don Kelley for a time such as this. Due largely to his effective leadership, the church remained focused and on track.

The newly elected pastor search committee consisted of three members: Shirley Beacham, Kerry Henderson and Mike Sweet.

In late spring 2001, it was announced to the church that the committee was recommending Dr. Drew Hines to be the next pastor of Washington.

DR. DREW HINES
(2001-Present)

Dr. Drew Hines

Drew Hines was born in Greensboro, North Carolina and lived there until he and his parents moved to Greenville, South Carolina, in late 1969. He graduated from Wade Hampton High School, the University of South Carolina in Columbia, and Southern Baptist Theological Seminary in Louisville, Kentucky, with Master of Divinity and Doctor of Ministry degrees. His previous pastorates included Foster Avenue Baptist Church in Louisville, Ebenezer Welcome Baptist Church in Landrum, Pleasant Grove Baptist Church in Greer, and the First Baptist Church of Andrews, South Carolina. He also served the denomination as director of missions for the Moriah Baptist Association in Lancaster, South Carolina, and as director of pastoral ministries for the South Carolina Baptist Convention in Columbia.

He has been married to the former Suzanne Morris since August 16, 1976, and they are parents of two children, Miranda and Andrew, and at this writing they have four grandchildren.

After a unanimous call, Hines officially began his ministry at Washington on June 8, 2001. When he arrived, he found a church that was strong, unified and ready to go to work.

The supporting staff at Washington when the new pastor started his work included: Karla Ross, minister of music; Angie Huskey, church secretary; and Joe Henderson, church custodian. Robin Carlisle had taken a brief break from serving as the church's minister of youth, but he would return to those duties just a few months after Hines arrived.

JOE HENDERSON
(Custodian)

Joe Henderson

Joe Henderson worked many years as Washington's custodian. A lifelong member of the church, he and his wife, Barbara, served the congregation in many different capacities down through the years. Joe was a deacon, and Barbara was Sunday school director for nearly two decades. Joe and Barbara were the parents of Kerry Henderson who, along with his wife, Neltia, have worked for several years as missionaries, both at home and abroad.

Joe Henderson served the church as custodian faithfully until his death in 2010.

BETTY LYNN
(Church Secretary)

In 2002, the church welcomed a new member to the staff. Mrs. Betty Hendrix Lynn became church secretary and served faithfully for six years. Her professional competence, along with her helpful and congenial personality, made her an important part of the life of Washington. Betty

Betty Lynn

and her husband, Buddy, make their home in Greer and are active members of their church. Soon after Betty Lynn's retirement, the church hired Mrs. Dana Salsman as their new secretary.

DANA SALSMAN
(Church Secretary)

Dana and her husband, Les, are faithful members of Apalache Baptist Church. The couple have two sons and one granddaughter. Dana handles her many responsibilities with great skill and patience. When church members come by the office or call, they know they will be met by someone who will always offer a smile, a friendly word, and competent assistance.

Dana is assisted by Mrs. Sherry Smith, who joined the staff on a part-time basis in 2019 following the resignation of Mrs. Allison Grubbs, who had earlier served faithfully in that same position. Washington Baptist Church is truly blessed to have committed and capable support staff.

On September 11, 2001, a tragic and momentous event occurred as Muslim terrorists flew two jetliners into the World Trade Center, one into

Dana Salsman

the Pentagon, and another crashing in a field in Pennsylvania. This vicious attack on American soil opened the eyes of many to the impending dangers of domestic terrorism. No longer did Americans feel safe and secure in their own country. And yet, on a positive note, many Americans realized their true dependence on God for safety and security. A spiritual awakening of sorts resulted from this terrible national crisis. On the evening of September 11, Pastor Hines called the church and community to prayer. A large number of people congregated in the sanctuary to pray and seek God during this tumultuous and life-changing moment.

Gradually, the church began to grow. A watershed event for Washington was the creation of a strategic planning committee consisting of eleven elected members, plus the staff and department heads.

The committee met at Camp Marietta in August 2002 for a weekend retreat of prayer and planning. Together, they developed a vision statement, later approved by the church and still used to this day. It declares:

> "Washington Baptist Church is a family
> of committed believers linked by love,
> and dedicated to sharing Christ
> with our community and the world."

This vision statement first appeared on the front of *The Washington Window*, on September 1, 2002, and appears on every masthead that's currently published.

Many needs were first identified by this 2002 study group, but two stood out in particular. The first was the need for additional staff. As the church continued to grow, it was clear that more help was necessary.

The other need identified was in the area of facilities. It became apparent that if the church continued in its growth, there would soon be a lack of space.

In terms of additional staff, there was some uncertainty about where this staff member would be needed the most. The committee and the deacons pledged to pray, and God acted.

REV. JOE PRICE
(Associate Pastor, 2004-Present)

Rev. Joe Price

In March 2004, Joe Price made an appointment with Pastor Hines to discuss his future. God was working in his life, and Price felt that God might be leading him in a totally new direction professionally. A native of Greer, Joe is a graduate of Clemson University, and a lifelong member of Apalache Baptist Church. He is a deeply committed Christian who served the Lord faithfully at Apalache in a number of capacities.

His wife, the former Drenda Gibson, had been a member of Washington before they married. They are the parents of two children, Martin and Katie, and they have one grandchild.

Joe identifies three monumental events that he deems life-changing. The first was his introduction to Henry Blackaby's *Experiencing God* Bible study. This study has played a huge role in the spiritual growth of Washington Baptist Church down through the years. Then, a mission trip to Romania opened his eyes to the world's vast need for Christ. Also, his early involvement in the Release Time ministry in Greer has been an important reminder to him of God's power and ability.

After their initial meeting together, both Pastor Hines and Joe Price agreed to pray. Joe had no idea that the strategic planning committee was exploring the option of adding another staff member. As the pastor prayed, it became clear that God could be opening the door for Joe to come on board in a full-time capacity. As the church grew, the need was quickly arising for an ongoing program of education and discipleship. It seemed that Joe's gifts of teaching and administration were perfect to fit this need. The church approved, and Joe began his duties during the last week of July 2004. Apalache Baptist Church ordained him, and he has served the Lord and His church faithfully and with distinction.

The other area of concern was the need for additional space, and this was initially addressed by the church in 2005. Early in 2006, the congregation agreed to further explore the possibility of expansion, particularly the addition of much-needed educational space. A building committee was elected, and Alan Edney, who also served as church treasurer, was elected chairman of the group. It was soon decided that Steve Newton, architect with LifeWay Church

On October 3, 2006, Washington voted to proceed with the construction of the new facility at a cost of $2.4 million.

Resources in Nashville, should be invited to come and meet with this committee to make a recommendation. After that first meeting, Newton created several preliminary drawings that seemed to perfectly suit the future needs of the church. SYS Construction Company, of Greenville, was commissioned by the congregation to be the chief contractor of the project. On October 3, 2006, the church voted to proceed with the

Demolition of the old church sanctuary and education building.

construction of the new facility at a cost of $2.4 million. However, in order to construct a new building, an old one had to be demolished.

It was a sad day for many when, on March 12, 2007, demolition of the 1899-era sanctuary and educational building was begun.

Before the final demolition, the bricks were removed from the old building revealing the original weather boarding. It looked eerily like the building when it was first constructed in the late nineteenth century. For the sake of progress, this edifice soon disappeared to make way for the spacious facility the church enjoys today.

In the middle of this ambitious building project, 2.66 acres of land became available directly behind the church. Because of its location, it made perfect sense for the church to purchase it — but should Washington make such a bold move right in the middle of a multi-million-dollar building program? The cost was a modest $75,000 and, thankfully, it was decided to proceed with their purchase. God blessed in this decision, because only after the sale did the project engineers reveal that the purchase of this property would have been necessary to accommodate the size of the septic system needed for the building expansion. Once again, the Lord had proved His faithfulness to Washington Baptist Church!

It was a glorious day in the life of the church when, on January 27, 2008, the Washington family dedicated its new facility. The service drew an audience from the entire community — and the newly added offices, Sunday school rooms, nursery and preschool facilities, along with a new youth area, were admired by all. It was with great gratitude to God that the doors opened and the area was put to good use. Within five years, the entire debt for the construction would be paid. No one could have

Dedication of the new Washington facilities. Presenting the keys to the building are trustees (left to right): Don Black, Ronnie Knight, Tom Beacham, and Alan Edney, chairman of the building committee.

imagined that the church would once again be debt free so quickly!

AWANA
(2005-Present)

Another landmark event in the history of Washington Baptist Church was the beginning of AWANA in 2005. AWANA, which stands for Approved Workers Are Not Ashamed, has historically been an effective program of Bible teaching and discipleship for children featuring scripture memorization, instruction in the Bible, and action-packed games. The idea was first introduced by some members who were familiar with AWANA's success in other settings and thought that it might play an important role in the spiritual growth of Washington's children. Tara Walker was Washington's first AWANA commander, and she served faithfully in that capacity for several years. Heidi Mangum is

Sharlee Lindley teaches AWANA Cubbies during puppet time.

Just a few of the Washington GAs.
(back row, left to right): Leaders Jennifer Steadman, Jessica O'Bryant,
Keri Hanley, and Nan Spearman;
(middle row, left to right): Maddisyn Hanley, Macie Hanley,
and Emily Underwood
(front row, left to right): Emmie O'Bryant, Bella Van Patton,
and Lilla Steadman.

the current AWANA commander, and the church continues, after nearly fifteen years, to see wonderful results in the lives of young people.

Since the church's early days, GAs (Girls in Action), RAs (Royal Ambassadors), and Mission Friends have also been a critical component of the education and spiritual growth of Washington's children. These three ministries are primarily outlets for mission education of Southern Baptist children. Generations of young people have learned of God's activity around the world through the efforts of Southern Baptist missionaries. Without a doubt, many who are serving as missionaries today first learned of God's great work around the world through GAs,

RAs at Camp McCall 2017 (left to right): Noah Baker, Chase Barbare, Austin Steadman, Jake Ayers, Nathan Hudson, and Hank Lee.

RAs and Mission Friends. AWANA meets on Sunday evenings, and RAs, GAs and Mission Friends meet on Wednesday evenings. Washington hosts Vacation Bible School in the summer with Mrs. Melanie Hughes serving as director. Also, in the summer, the church sponsors SAM camp, which presents the Gospel to children through sports, art and music.

Speaking of missions, Washington has long taken a "hands on" approach to mission work. In 2002, the church entered into a partnership with the Iglesia Tabernaculo Church in Managua, Nicaragua. For some time, church members had been actively involved in the Chosen Children ministry to Nicaragua. This was a ministry primarily focused on a children's home in Managua. Several trips to this facility had been made by Washington members, and much good had been accomplished in the name of Christ. One of the most frequently visited churches during these trips was the Iglesia Tabernaculo. A friendship had been forged with Pastor José and the members of his congregation. After an exploratory trip was made by Pastor Drew Hines and mission director

Tony Wallace to Managua, the two churches agreed to enter into a five-year partnership. During this time, frequent trips were made to Nicaragua for construction projects, community Vacation Bible Schools, and fellowship and encouragement. This was an important period of growth and further commitment to missions for Washington.

Much closer to home, on July 9-13, 2008, Washington took a very important mission trip to Jonesville, Virginia, led by then North American Missions director Mike O'Bryant. It was during this historic week that the church identified several areas of need in this impoverished corner of Virginia. This region, once home to numerous coal mines which were, at one time, the chief employers of area residents, was now economically depressed because of the closing of those mines in recent

Lee County Virginia mission team (back row, left to right):
North American Mission director Mike O'Bryant, Ben Dryden,
Wyatt Spearman, Suzanne Spearman, Drew Hines,
Joe Price, Joel Morris, Trey Frick, and Jill Frick.
(front row, left to right): Sandra O'Bryant, Karla Ross,
Cheryl Moore, Lauren Dryden, Meredith Frick,
Emily Underwood, and Rhonda Underwood.

years. The church made a commitment to assist these people any way possible. It all began with a partnership of sorts with Darbyville Baptist Church in Lee County, Virginia. Pastor Earnie Bledsoe and the people of Darbyville have welcomed Washington members with open arms into their church and into their hearts. Important work has been done, and lifelong friendships have been forged.

Several different construction projects have been initiated down through the years — most recently, the installation of a new baptistry in the church. There have been evangelistic crusades, Vacation Bible Schools and other projects in the area, including an ongoing outreach to Chestnut Grove, a facility housing mentally challenged adults. Every year around Christmas, several members of Washington, both young and old, visit Chestnut Grove, bringing Christmas presents to each resident and having a program of holiday music. Homemade snacks are also distributed at this party. Both visitors and residents look forward to this festive annual holiday tradition. Mr. David Underwood, who also leads men's ministries at Washington, plans and coordinates much of the work in Virginia.

2002 Washington mission team to Nicaragua.

TRAVIS HENSON
(Part-Time Minister of Youth, 2005-Present)

Travis Henson

In November 2005, the church called Travis Henson to be their part-time minister of youth. Travis, the son of Jerry and Linda Henson, is a native of the Blue Ridge area, graduating from Blue Ridge High School and the University of South Carolina-Upstate.

Travis has taught in the school systems of Greenville and Spartanburg counties for a number of years, and has also coached baseball on the high school and college level (North Greenville University). Several of his teams have won championships during his tenure. Travis has, over the years, also been a very popular speaker for youth and athletic teams all across the area.

The relationship between Pastor Hines and Travis Henson goes back to Hines' days as pastor of Ebenezer Welcome Baptist Church in Landrum in the early 1980s. Ebenezer Welcome is Travis' home church, and he was baptized by Pastor Hines. Years later, after Robin Carlisle's resignation as Washington's minister of youth, Travis and Drew's paths crossed once again, and the Lord led Travis into the youth leadership position at Washington. The Lord has used him mightily over the years to inspire and motivate not only the youth of this church, but young people throughout the community.

On August 4, 2007, Travis married Jennifer Smith of Williamston. A graduate of Clemson University, Jennifer is also a teacher and has been a coach throughout the years. Together, Travis and Jennifer have made important contributions to the lives of many young people, as well as being wonderful assets to the church in general.

Since the year 2000, the church has annually hosted a conference for the women of the church and community. This conference features

Youth mission trip to Lakewood Campground in Myrtle Beach,
July 2019. Pictured are (back row, left to right): Emma Kate Edwards,
Brooke Edwards, Kaleb Edwards, and Ashlynne Boone.
(middle row, left to right): Keliah Walker, Lauren Dryden,
and Samantha Styles.
(front row, left to right): Nolan Hudson, Caroline Frick,
Brooklyn Higginbotham, Wyatt Spearman, and S.J. Boone.

One of the many beautifully decorated tables at Washington's annual Women's Conference.

inspirational music and an uplifting message delivered by an invited speaker. A delicious meal is always served, but one of the highlights of this event are the beautifully decorated tables created by table hostesses. The best china, crystal and silverware are used, and the men of the church serve as waiters for the evening. Over the years, this banquet has been held in the family life center of the church, but in April 2019, the church's new fellowship hall was used and served as a beautiful and very convenient venue for this ever-popular event.

THE WASHINGTON BELLES

Still another amazing testimony of God's faithfulness is the story of the handbell choir of Washington Baptist Church, better known as the "Washington Belles."

The Washington Belles, 2009.
Pictured (left to right): Jennifer Steadman, Iris LeCren, Toni Arms,
Drenda Price, Jenna Leigh Church, Kristi Mathis, Anita Ayers,
Tracie Carlisle, Karla Ross, and director Jackie Church.

This story begins in September 2009, when Mrs. Jackie Church first met with the pastor to discuss the possibility of organizing a hand bell choir. She had participated in this ministry in another church and felt the Lord might be directing her to start one at Washington. At the time, the cost of the bells seemed prohibitive, and both Jackie and Pastor Hines agreed to pray about the matter. In the meantime, the church was mourning the loss of one of its most faithful members, Mrs. Doris Howell. Mrs. Howell, along with her husband, Mac, and two sons, Tim and Jeff, had been a part of the Washington family for many years. Doris' younger son Jeff and his wife, Nella, had joined Greer's First Presbyterian Church, which had an active and accomplished hand bell choir.

After Mrs. Howell's death, Jeff made an appointment with Pastor Hines to discuss the possibility of using memorial funds, along with a generous contribution from the family, to purchase hand bells in memory of his mother. Having no knowledge of the pastor's earlier conversations with Jackie Church, this seemed to confirm the leadership of the Lord. And so on April 25, 2010, with Mrs. Doris Howell's family present, the church dedicated a beautiful set of hand bells in her memory and to the glory of God. The "Washington Belles" were organized under the direction of Mrs. Jackie Church, and have, ever since, been a very important part of the ongoing worship of Washington Baptist Church.

Another generous gift to the church at about this same time has benefited the whole Washington community in a beautiful way. In 2011, Mr. and Mrs. Ronnie Knight donated a carillon system to the church in memory of their parents — Riley Ray and Cornelia Ray Gaston, and Wales and Ora Dell Knight. As a result of this gift, beautiful sacred music is broadcast three times daily across the countryside from the Washington steeple, bringing great pleasure and inspiration to all who hear.

HOLIDAY TRADITIONS

Traditions are very important to people, and there have been a few established over the years at Washington that have left their mark.

One event that has been around for many years now is the annual Easter sunrise service. Usually beginning at seven a.m. on Easter morning, this service is held outside, weather permitting. For several years, worshipers gathered at the Lake Robinson picnic shelter, and it was a lovely setting. However, after the construction of the church's picnic shelter, the service has been there ever since. A breakfast follows, hosted and served by the deacons and their wives. This is a perfect way to usher in the celebration of our Lord's glorious resurrection.

Another annual tradition that is a favorite with the church, as well as the community, is the "Amazing Autumn Celebration." Held every year on Halloween, members of the church volunteer to have treats for trick-or-treaters in the trunks of their vehicles in the church's parking lot. Hot dogs are served in the family life center and various games are played that attract the young and the young at heart. This annual celebration has become a tremendous outreach tool for the church, as many as 1,000 hot dogs have been served on this special night. For several years, Mrs. Melanie Hughes has overseen the autumn celebration. She has also served as Vacation Bible School director as well as leading a variety of women's Bible studies.

Every Wednesday before Thanksgiving, the congregation gathers in the fellowship hall for the annual pre-Thanksgiving pinto bean supper. This tradition was established shortly after Pastor Hines arrived at Washington. It's a time of worship, thanksgiving, and, of course, great fellowship around the table.

As Christmas approaches, two more holiday traditions come around. On the evening of the first Sunday of Advent, Washington celebrates the "Hanging of the Green." On that evening, the sanctuary begins to take on the beauty of Christmas as wreaths are hung, garlands are strung, and trees and candles are lit. Throughout the hour, beautiful Christmas music is also presented by various groups within the church, along with Bible readings related to the celebration of Christmas. The "Hanging of the Green" has been an important part of Washington's Christmas observances since 2001. This event has been directed by Mrs. Patsy Tapp Edney since its inception.

Another wonderful Christmas tradition at Washington is the annual Christmas Eve service. The service, which begins promptly at 11 p.m. and ends at midnight, attracts people from the whole community. Beautiful music, along with a solemn and moving observance of the Lord's Supper, highlights this special event. Both the "Hanging of the Green" and the Christmas Eve service are two of the most popular and best-attended events of the entire year.

Other favorite Washington traditions include the annual ice cream fellowship held at the church's picnic shelter, usually in June or July, and the fall cookout, also at the picnic shelter in October. Both of these events are sponsored and hosted by the church's deacons.

As early as 2010, the church began considering the construction of a picnic shelter and outdoor recreation area. The 2.66 acres of land purchased by the church during the 2007-2008 building project seemed perfect for this area. Built almost entirely by volunteers from the church, both the picnic shelter and a beautiful playground for the children were constructed in 2012. On June 24, 2012, the picnic shelter was dedicated, and the first event held there was the annual ice cream fellowship. This lovely and spacious facility is used often and makes a perfect venue, not only for church-wide events, but also birthday parties, family reunions, picnics, and other family celebrations.

Later that summer, construction began on a children's playground behind the church and close to the picnic shelter. Once again, volunteers from the church stepped up and completed the work. By September, children were enjoying this new recreational facility.

Thank you to Vivian Langford, who compiled this list:

Keith Armstrong	Brad Ridings — grading
Jackie Barton	Eddie Smith
Tony Black	Philip Stevenson
Todd Bruce	Bill Thompson
Steve Church	Wanda Vaughn
Chad Cooper	Rex Wilbanks
Carroll Crawford	Doug Walker
Stuart Liddell	Frank Hawkins
Albert McAbee	Lou Ellen Barnette
Linda McAbee	Don Black
Mike O'Bryant	Ricky Bradshaw
Dwayne Pack — labor	Jack Camp

Brian Cooper

Bill Crawford

Ben Dryden

Brent Lindley

Bud McAbee

Chris O'Bryant

Rod Owens — crane

Todd Ponder

Dennis Schneider

Greg Spearman

Lamar Sudduth

Richard Vaughn

Greg Weaver

Ben Edwards — sod

Dustin Ross

The year 2012 closed on an incredibly positive note, as the Lord has provided for the church in a miraculous way.

During the expansion and building process of 2007-2008, the church's architect, Steve Newton, shared with church leaders that, should more building be needed in the future, the property adjacent to the

Washington children enjoy their new playground.

Washington's picnic shelter is a wonderful place for outdoor fellowship.

church — bordering on Bomar Road — would be very valuable, if not necessary, to accommodate the expansion. The property, containing 3.2 acres, and owned by Fred and Sheila Ross, was not for sale at a price the church felt it could afford at that time. In the meantime, a conversation was initiated with the pastor by Mr. Philip Bradshaw, a former church member and son of the late Ray and Christine Bomar Bradshaw. Mr. Bradshaw offered to give the church the amount necessary to purchase the property — and the church agreed to accept his very kind and generous gift. On December 30, 2012, in a special called business meeting, the church voted to purchase the Ross property consisting of a house, a large workshop/building and 3.2 acres of land, at a cost of $300,000. Later, the house was demolished and the land graded. The workshop building has been preserved and houses the church's golf carts.

More opportunity for ministry emerged in 2013 in an area no one had previously imagined. Church member Ross Burgess met with the pastor and associate pastor to discuss the possibility of beginning a motorcycle ministry in the church. He spoke of all the church members

The Faith Riders embarking on another road trip for Christ.

who were bikers and the open doors of evangelism and ministry to a group outside the church that was largely unreached. After much prayer and consideration, the Faith Riders were soon organized with Ross Burgess and John Forrester, leading the group in road trips, charity events, and evangelistic activities. The Resurrection Ride, an annual activity leading up to Easter, has been a signature event for this group, drawing many from outside the church. Also, every year the group has participated in the Shoebox ministry of Samaritan's Purse in Charlotte. They pack up and take these gifts to the headquarters, where they will soon be distributed around the world. The Faith Riders have since evolved into the Rolling Church, and they continue to make an impact in their community.

A NEW ASSOCIATION

Washington Baptist Church has always, during its 200 years of existence, been actively involved in denominational activities. From the national convention to the South Carolina Baptist Convention, and all the way down to the local association, the church has banded together with other churches to reach the world for Christ.

Through the years, Washington has been a part of several associations. In 1959, the congregation became a founding member of the Greer Baptist Association and faithfully served and contributed to that body for fifty-four years. In 2013, talks began between the Greer Baptist Association and the North Greenville Baptist Association about the possibility of merging the two groups together. After much prayer and deliberation, this dream became a reality, and on October 20, 2013, the newly formed Three Rivers Baptist Association met for the first time. As it had been in the Greer Association, Washington had the distinction of being a charter member of this group. Dr. Randy Bradley, former director of missions in the North Greenville Baptist Association, became Three Rivers' first director of missions — while Rev. Tom Capps, former director of missions for the Greer Association, became the group's director of missions ministries. The new association built its offices and mission center on Locust Hill Road in the Sandy Flat community. Washington contributed, both financially and with much volunteer labor, in the construction of this beautiful facility. On October 13, 2019, the church was delighted to be able to host the Three Rivers Baptist Association in its annual meeting.

> **On October 20, 2013, the newly formed Three Rivers Baptist Association met for the first time.**

In 2013, Washington made another very important decision with the creation of the Canaan committee. Two previous long-range planning groups had led the church into making some very important and historical decisions. In 2013, the pastor recommended the organization of another committee he called the Canaan committee, harking back to the time when the Israelites made the decision to advance into the land of Canaan. Canaan was God's land of promise for them. Pastor Hines felt that the best days of Washington lay just ahead in their very own Canaan.

The church elected members to serve on this committee, and a retreat was held January 31-February 1, 2014, in which the group prayed and deliberated together about the future course Washington should take. Strengths and weaknesses were identified. As a result of this weekend retreat, the committee recommended the formation of four subcommittees to tackle what was felt to be some of the church's major challenges. Those subcommittees were:

Evangelism   Missions/Ministry

Facilities   Worship

Mrs. Cheryl Moore was chosen to lead this group, and they immediately began their work. Some of this group's accomplishments down through the years include:

1. The recommendation to build more facilities.
2. SAM Camp — an annual children's event for grades 1-6 which highlights sports, art and music with an emphasis on the presentation of the Gospel.
3. Children's summer activities.
4. Hiring Mrs. Toni Arms as children's minister.
5. Creation of the live-stream broadcast of church services.
6. Block parties.
7. Car shows.
8. New member Sunday school class.
9. *Gripped by the Greatness of God* Bible study.
10. Follow-up with families from Amazing Autumn Celebration

and SAM Camp.

11. Starting Washington 101.

As many of these recommendations have been implemented and the church has seen some very visible and positive results, it just seems to be further confirmation of the Lord's leadership.

One of the areas of need identified was the creation of a part-time position to deal with ministry to children. For many years, one of the strong points of Washington has been its effective outreach to children through many different means, including:

Sunday school	GAs
Vacation Bible School	Mission Friends
AWANA	Children's Choirs
RAs	SAM Camp

This was all led by dedicated, committed volunteers, but many felt a part-time staff position for children's ministries would concentrate and coordinate this program in a greater way. It became the recommendation of the Canaan committee that this position be created. After much prayer and discussion, an independent committee designed for this search recommended that Mrs. Toni Arms become Washington's first children's minister.

TONI ARMS
(Children's Minister, 2017-Present)

In June of 2017, Toni Arms officially began her duties. Toni, a native of Greer, was also a product of Victor Baptist Church. She married Mike Arms and joined Washington, her husband's home church, and has

Toni Arms

remained a faithful and involved member of this congregation. It became apparent early on that she had a burden for children, and she served in many different capacities of children's ministry before her call to this position. Mike and Toni have two sons, Josh and Brad, and five grandchildren.

On May 2, 2014, the congregation was notified that the entire estate of Mrs. Nell Lister Few had been given to Washington Baptist Church. This estate included just over thirty acres of land located at 2308 East Gap Creek Road, along with cash and personal property totaling $247,691.86.

Mrs. Few and her family had long been faithful members of Washington, and the impact of this one lady's very generous gift will be felt for generations to come.

Still more property became available to the church in 2014, when it was announced that the estate of Mr. Andrew George would be sold at auction on November 18, 2014. This property just north and adjacent to the church consisted of a house, several outbuildings and 5.8 acres of land.

Originally a part of the old Bomar property, the stately two-story house was built in 1861. On November 2, 2014, in conference, the church agreed to let Mr. Ronnie Knight serve as their agent and purchase the property by bid. The purchase price at auction was $179,300. Currently, the church's clothing closet is housed in the old George home.

It should be mentioned that during all this busy financial activity, Mr.

Stuart Williams has served faithfully and well as Washington's church treasurer. For several years, Mr. Alan Edney had filled that role with distinction. In the critical days during the first expansion, Mr. Edney was not only the treasurer, but he was also chairman of the building committee. Shortly before his untimely death in September 2012, he expressed the desire to train someone to step into his place should that become necessary. Stuart Williams was tapped to succeed Alan as treasurer. He was trained and ready when needed, and he has served in that capacity ever since. The role of church treasurer has grown as the church membership has increased. It is a tremendous responsibility, and Stuart's tenure in that role has been remarkable and commendable.

Further building expansion was on the horizon! As early as 2015, the facility subcommittee of the Canaan committee was busy making recommendations about the need for expansion. The church was kept well-informed about the findings of this committee and the preliminary steps to proceed. Indeed, in 2015 these were "baby steps." However, a huge step of faith was taken by the church on August 30, 2015, when in conference the church elected a building committee. Members of this group included:

Richard Vaughn, chairman	Ronnie Knight
Tracie Carlisle	Cheryl Moore
Scott Chisam	Bonnie Mussman
Rusty Edwards	Lamar Sudduth
Kenny Hughes	

From October 2015, through the summer of 2016, many preliminary decisions were made by the building committee. Once again, Washington called upon Steve Newton of Nashville to serve as chief architect for this project. Newton had left his position as architect with the Southern

Baptist Sunday School Board and had begun his own firm. His partner, Gary Nicholson, would be included in on the Washington project. From their initial meeting on October 28, 2015, the building committee had pretty much determined the greatest need in this facility expansion was for more Sunday school space, along with a large fellowship hall and an area for the food pantry.

It was indeed a historical day in the life of Washington Baptist Church when, on Sunday morning, March 19, 2017, the congregation voted to proceed in earnest with the new building addition. At that time, it was estimated the total cost of this project would be $4.3 million. Mr. Ronnie Knight presented a proposal that the church borrow $3.4 million from GrandSouth Bank. After much discussion, the church voted by secret ballot, and results were 376 in favor of proceeding and 13 against. Clayton Construction Company of Greenville, South Carolina

Groundbreaking for Washington's new building addition.

was selected to oversee the construction, with Mr. F.M. Elliott, former member of Washington, to be project foreman.

On Sunday morning, April 30, 2017, the church family gathered behind the church on the construction site for a groundbreaking ceremony. The youngest baptized member of the church at that time, Lilla Steadman, along with the church's oldest member, Mrs. Sarah Tolbert, who was ninety-nine, were selected to serve in the groundbreaking ceremony. Dr. Randy Bradley, director of missions for the Three Rivers Baptist Association, was also present and participated. Mr. Harry Clayton, president of Clayton Construction, and Mr. F.M. Elliott, foreman of the project, were also participants in this special event, along with the church building committee.

The building project proceeded in earnest after ground was broken and, for the most part, went smoothly. The church watched with excitement and anticipation as the building construction came together.

NEW FACILITY
(2017-2018)

It was a day of celebration when finally, after nearly nineteen months of construction, the church was able to dedicate their new facilities. Dedication took place on November 18, 2018, during the 10:45 a.m. worship service. Mrs. Vivian Langford summarized the day:

> "Eleven years after the first Sunday school
> complex was added to Washington Church,
> the church had grown in number so much that
> another addition was needed. The long range
> planning committee began to meet, to pray,
> and to seek the Lord's guidance for the future of

the church. Plans were made and presented to the church, and the work began. The work was slow but was led by the Lord. As the building was put together, the members were given an opportunity to sign an interior beam of the church. In future years, if this beam is exposed for any reason, the member names will be recognized. This dedication service was held in the beautiful new fellowship room of the church.

The service was opened in prayer by Travis Henson, minister of youth. After the prayer, the doxology was sung by the entire assembly of people. The theme of the service was 'To God Be The Glory,' as this was indeed a work and blessing of God. Invocation was given by Rev. Joe Price, assistant pastor. Special music was presented by Trey Frick, Karla Ross, and Tracie Carlisle. The congregation then sang a hymn, 'Let There Be Glory and Honor and Praise,' followed by responsive reading. The offering was taken with a hymn being sung 'To God Be the Glory,' as Debbie Burden, the pianist, played beautiful music. The choir then sang 'Cornerstone.' This song was also sung at the dedication of the new Sunday school addition in 2007. Mr. Kenny Hughes, member of the building committee, made a short talk, thanking the committee and telling how the building came together under the Lord's direction.

Dr. Drew Hines had a short but very good message using 1 Chronicles 29:10-15, praising

the Lord for His goodness. Invitation was given.
The evening service was one of celebration of
fellowship held in the new building."

The new facilities have been put to good use since the congregation first occupied them in November, 2018. The new fellowship hall with its beautiful, modern kitchen has become home to weekly Wednesday night suppers, and the annual Ladies Banquet found it more than adequate to host this event for the first time in April 2019.

The new Sunday school classes are a welcome addition and have made it possible for new classes to be started. Another advantage of the additional space has been the creation of an area totally devoted to preschoolers and children.

All adult classes that were meeting on the main level of the 2007 addition, moved to the new Sunday school area making available extra space near the nursery and preschool classes. The decision was made to consolidate all the children's classes into this part of the building. As a result, the area was renovated and dedicated to children's ministry.

Washington's new fellowship hall, November 18, 2018.

Washington's new Sunday school addition.

Beautiful artwork for the area was designed by Mrs. Candace Rathbone, along with creative stenciling and artwork by Mrs. Sandra O'Bryant, Mrs. Amanda Van Patton and Mrs. Jessica O'Bryant. The wing was soon dedicated and put to good use. It's attractive, spacious, secure, and has been a great addition to the children's outreach and discipleship.

The bottom floor of this building has been dedicated entirely to the church's food pantry and for use in other mission/ministry efforts.

Washington's new children's department wing.

THE FOOD PANTRY

This valuable area of ministry began in the hearts of some of Washington's members who saw a need in the community and desired to meet that need. Local missions director, Josh Harvey, first envisioned a way to reach hungry people at their greatest point of need. Working with missions director David O'Shields, the Washington food pantry was born on Saturday, September 17, 2011. Every Saturday morning since its opening, between 50 and 100 people have come seeking assistance. There are two requirements they must fulfill. First, recipients must register so the church will have a record of who is attending, and, especially, who is seeking help on a consistent basis. These people are also given the opportunity to share prayer requests, and these prayer requests are distributed so church members can regularly pray for these needs. The second requirement is that those seeking help first listen to a devotional prepared and delivered by a member of the church. These devotionals/sermons are helpful and challenging, and always have an

Washington's food pantry and assembly room.

evangelistic emphasis.

Food from the food pantry is both donated by Washington members and purchased by the church through outlets such as Harvest Hope Food Bank. Those seeking the food pantry's assistance on Saturdays are given bags of groceries and produce that are both delicious and nutritious.

Along with the food pantry, a clothing closet ministry is offered to those who receive food assistance. Volunteers work tirelessly to prepare the clothing and categorize by size so it can be made readily available to those arriving after the food pantry time. The clothing closet is housed at the George property and has also become a valuable ministry and outreach tool for the church.

So with these vital and important ministry and mission tools in place Washington enters its third century of existence with vision and purpose. To facilitate this progress and growth, God has put together a staff that continues to serve Him faithfully and well into the future.

As of 2019, the current Washington ministerial and support staff includes:

Drew Hines — Pastor

Joe Price — Associate Pastor

Karla Ross — Minister of Music

Travis Henson — Minister of Youth

Toni Arms — Minister of Children

Debbie Rigsby — Pianist

Lydia Waddell — Organist

Dana Salsman — Administrative Assistant

Sherry Smith — Administrative Assistant, part-time

Cesar Vaccari — Custodian

Karen Cobb — Custodian

Paul and Lisa Bracewell — Sexton

FORWARD BY FAITH

What does the future hold for Washington Baptist Church? We may not know what tomorrow holds, but as the old Gospel song expresses, we do know who holds tomorrow. And thus, Washington Baptist Church, as it has for 200 years, goes forward by faith. Surely there will be challenges, as there have always been in the past, but still we move ahead in the name of Jesus! We are linked by faith and love.

Faith and love are the keys to any church's success. They both are timeless in their importance and effect. They work well, whether the year is 1819 or 2019. Hebrews 11:6 says, "But without faith it is impossible to please God." A church that inches along by sight instead of stepping out boldly by faith will remain a shell of what God desires it to be. Washington members have seen over the years that the church must respond positively and believe God as the Lord extends tests of faith. Faith is the life blood of the church. When a church stops believing, they stop living.

The other key component is love. According to Jesus, love is the identifying badge of the church. He said in John 13:35, "By this shall all men know that ye are my disciples, if ye have love one to another." Love draws people. Where people feel love and acceptance, it is there they tend to gather. Washington is a place where people have experienced the love of Jesus for 200 years, and it must continue, if the Lord tarries, for 200 more!

To underscore this point, I wish to bring this book to a conclusion with a poem written by the late Joe Ross, a longtime member of Washington Baptist Church. This poem was written on the occasion of Washington's 150th anniversary and was published in *The Washington Window* on October 19, 1969. It is entitled, most appropriately, "A Church Built on Love":

If we could go back 150 years (or 200)
We would all probably be in tears.
The world has changed in so many ways
But I've noticed God's love just
Stays and stays.
This is why we have a church today
Some came and went, others decided to stay.
But working together because of love
We have survived the devil's big shove.
Jesus warned about building on sand
And also that He will come again.
Washington found a rock and started to build.
Only after they had prayed and found His will.
There were those who gave all they had
And others who criticized and said it was bad.
Only with hand in hand and heart to heart
Can we have a church the devil can't tear apart.
So when we've been there ten thousand years
We can look back without shedding tears.
Yes, we can look and see His land and say
We know His church is standing today.
Because it was ordained from above,
And built on LOVE.

APPENDIX I
Pastors of Washington Baptist Church

Isaac Lamance (1819-1838)

Jesse Center (1838-1839)

Samuel Gibson (1840-1843)

Richard Woodruff (1844-1847)

Jefferson Barton (1848-1850)

Richard Webb (1850-1852)

Richard Woodruff (1852-1853)

Samuel Gibson (1853-1854)

Richard Woodruff (1854-1857)

S.T. Dill (1858-1865)

T.J. Earle (1866-1867)

Martin Van Buren Lankford (1868-1870)

Richard Furman Whilden (1870)

A.D. Bowers (1871)

Jason Hudson (1872-1875)

Richard Furman Whilden (1876)

Ludwell Vaughan (1877-1883)

S.T. Dill (1884-1886)

Jesse M. Allen (1887)

P.D. Green (1888)

J.R. Aiken (1888-1892)

J.L. Freeman (1893-1895)

D.P. Montgomery (1895-1896)

J.E. McManaway (1897-1908)

Harry Lee Riley (1908-1910)

W.P. Holland (1910)

J. Dean Crain (1911-1912)

W.J. Bolt (1913-1916)

M.B. Buckley (1916-1917)

Arthur L. Vaughn (1918-1919)

Samuel P. Cogburn (1919-1926)

Henry Clayton Hester (1927-1928)

Shields T. Hardin (1928-1931)

L.B. White (1932-1938)

Dwight L. Bragg (1938-1942)

O.B. Lancaster (1942-1952)

E.B. Lowery (1953-1955)

William M. King (1955-1959)

Kenneth M. Newton (1959-1972)

John B. Compton (1972-1977)

William M. Cashion (1978-1985)

Jim Ramsey (1987-1996)

Ron Bryan (1997-1999)

Drew Hines (2001-present)

APPENDIX II
Ministers of Music

For much of Washington's 200-year history, the role of minister of music was a volunteer position. Unfortunately, many of the names of those who served have been lost over time. Below are the names of those who can be remembered. Since the order and duration of their tenure is uncertain, their names have been alphabetized. Special thanks to Mrs. Elaine Huttenstine who assisted in gathering these names.

VOLUNTEERS

Charlie Belue

Luther Green

Davis Howard

Arthur Lynn

Lindsey Lynn

Fate Moon

PAID/ PART-TIME

Hugh Atkins

Charlie Clark

Harold Emmett

Alfred Garcia

Steve Gillespie

Stan Jones

Rick Knight

Bill Lee

Karla Ross

APPENDIX III
Deacons

The list below represents the deacons who have faithfully served Washington Baptist Church since 1957. Due to faulty record-keeping here and there, it has been impossible to put together a complete list of elected deacons prior to 1957. And even later in the last century, there are gaps, so the reader will notice some years left unrecorded. Many thanks to Mrs. Vivian Langford who, for the most part, compiled this list.

1957
Harold Hill
Lee Tolbert
Claude Brown
Marvin Wilson
Claudo Brown
Walter Atkins
Bill Gibson
Lindsay Lynn
Jimmy Barnett
George Holtzclaw
Worth Barnett

1958
Harold Hill
Darwin Gibson
Jimmy Barnett
Dan Ray Jr.
L.A. Lynn
Don Black

Hulon Lister
Dewey Turner
Claudo Brown
Lee Tolbert
Worth Barnett

1960

Worth Barnett
Marshall Burnette
Don Black
Hulon Lister
Luther Green
W.O. Durham
Keith Moore
Billy Wood
Dan Ray Jr.
Dewey Turner
Carroll Bomar
Hugh Brown

1961

Don Black
Hulon Lister
Luther Green
Worth Barnett
Marshall Burnette
Dan Ray Jr.
Dewey Turner
Carroll Bomar
Keith Moore
Billy Wood

1962

Darwin Gibson
Jimmy Barnett
James Ponder
W.O. Durham
L.A. Green
Worth Barnett
Hugh Brown
Paul Barton
Billy Wood
Keith Moore
Carroll Bomar

1963

Darwin Gibson
Billy Wood
Jimmy Barnett
Marshall Burnette
Keith Moore
Alvin Ponder
Harold Durham
Don Black
James Ponder
Worth Barnett
Bill Gibson
Paul Barton
Harold Hill
Hugh Brown

1964

Harold Hill

Ronnie Knight

Bill Gibson

Hugh Brown

James Ponder

Paul Barton

Keith Moore

Earl Waldrop

Willie Durham

Worth Barnett

Alvin Ponder

Marshall Burnette

Don Black

Harold Durham

Darwin Gibson

1965

Alvin Ponder

Hugh Brown

Ronnie Knight

Worth Barnett

Marshall Burnette

Earl Waldrop

Keith Moore

Don Black

Harold Durham

1966

Earl Waldrop

Don Black

Bill Gibson

Alvin Ponder

Joe Henderson

Marshall Burnette

Jimmy Barnett

Worth Barnett

Bill Merritt

Darwin Gibson

1967

Joe Henderson

Bill Gibson

Jimmy Barnett

Hugh Brown

J.C. Stephens

Alvin Ponder

Keith Moore

Darwin Gibson

Willie Durham

Manley Green

Bill Merritt

James Ponder

1968

Don Black
Manley Green
Alvin Ponder
Bill Gibson
Lee Styles
Hugh Brown
Darwin Gibson
Joe Henderson
Bill Merritt
J.C. Stephens

1969

Don Black
Hugh Brown
Manley Green
Earl Waldrop
J.C. Stephens
T.O. Sudduth
Claudo Brown
Paul Henderson
Alvin Ponder
Joe Henderson
Keith Moore
Hulon Arms

1970

Hulon Arms
Claudo Brown
Keith Moore

Marshall Burnette
J.C. Stephens
Manley Green
Bill Merritt
T.O. Sudduth
Earl Waldrop
Paul Henderson
Hugh Brown
Willie Durham

1971

Paul Henderson
Joe Henderson
Claudo Brown
Joe Ross
T.O. Sudduth
Bill Merritt
Alvin Ponder
Earl Waldrop
Marshall Burnette
Hulon Arms

1972

Don Black
Paul Barton
Joe Ross
Bill Merritt
Hugh Brown
T.O. Sudduth

Claudo Brown

Hulon Arms

Alvin Ponder

1973

Paul Henderson

Don Black

Hugh Brown

Keith Moore

Alvin Ponder

Paul Barton

Earl Waldrop

Joe Ross

Harold Durham

Willie Durham

Linny Moore

1974

Paul Henderson

Paul Barton

Claudo Brown

Keith Moore

T.O. Sudduth

Earl Waldrop

Willie Durham

Bill Merritt

Marshall Burnette

Hugh Brown

Linny Moore

1975

T.O. Sudduth

Claudo Brown

Dan Ray Jr.

Keith Moore

Linny Moore

Earl Waldrop

Bill Merritt

Paul Henderson

Don Black

Marshall Burnette

Alvin Ponder

1976

Dan Ray Jr.

Don Black

Hugh Brown

Darwin Gibson

Alvin Ponder

Melvin Murphy

Linny Moore

Joe Ross

Thurman Sudduth

1977

Don Black

Hugh Brown

Harold Durham

Darwin Gibson

Dan Lamb

T.O. Sudduth
Dan Ray Jr.
Keith Moore
Wilton Taylor
Willie Durham
Joe Ross
Alvin Ponder
Claudo Brown
Linny Moore

1978

Dan Lamb
Hugh Brown
Linny Moore
Melvin Murphy
T.O. Sudduth
Don Black
Bill Merritt
Keith Moore
Claudo Brown
Willie Durham
Marshall Burnette
Joe Ross
Earl Waldrop
Harold Durham

1979

Claudo Brown
Willie Durham
Linny Moore

Earl Waldrop
T.O. Sudduth
Don Black
Bill Merritt
Keith Moore
Harold Durham
Marshall Burnette
Dan Lamb

1980

Don Black
Linny Moore
Melvin Murphy
Earl Waldrop
Marshall Burnette
Harold Durham
Claudo Brown
Maurice Rice
Markley Edwards

1982

Linny Moore
James Pennington
Leon Kelly
Paul Barton
Markley Edwards
Melvin Murphy
Worth Barnett
Grover Jones
Richard Harvey

Danny Wilson
Keith Moore
Jimmy Sullivan
Maurice Rice
Joe Ross
Bill Gibson

1983

Kenny Hughes
Harold Fowler
Linny Moore
James Pennington
Jimmy Sullivan
Don Black
Joe Stokley
Richard Harvey
Danny Wilson

1996

Linny Moore
John Rainwater
Kerry Henderson
David O'Shields
Joe Aughtry
Gregg Moore
Markley Edwards
Don Black
Robin Carlisle
Bruce Durham

1997

Hulon Arms
Joe Aughtry
David O'Shields
Todd Ponder
Earl Rainey
Earl Waldrop
Bill Merritt
Gregg Moore
Robin Carlisle
Bruce Durham
Markley Edwards

1998

Hulon Arms
Joe Aughtry
Robin Carlisle
Bruce Durham
Markley Edwards
Kerry Henderson
Bill Merritt
Gregg Moore
David O'Shields
Todd Ponder
Earl Rainey
Earl Waldrop

1999

Joe Aughtry
Don Black

Robin Carlisle
Kerry Henderson
Linny Moore
David O'Shields
Bill Merritt
Mike O'Bryant
Earl Rainey
Mike Sweet
Earl Waldrop

2000
Hulon Arms
Don Black
Bruce Durham
Markley Edwards
Kerry Henderson
Gregg Moore
Linny Moore
Mike O'Bryant
David O'Shields
Mike Sweet
Tony Wallace

2001
Hulon Arms
Don Black
Bruce Durham
Markley Edwards
Kerry Henderson
Gregg Moore

Linny Moore
Mike O'Bryant
David O'Shields
Mike Sweet
Tony Wallace

2004
Chris Walker
Todd Ponder
Earl Waldrop
Ronnie Knight
Tom Beacham
Mike Sweet
Steve Cobb
Linny Moore
Don Black
Bill Merritt
Jackie Barton

2006
Don Black
Mike Sweet
Mike O'Bryant
Linny Moore
Earl Waldrop
Jackie Barton
Daniel Ross
Kenny Hughes
Steve Cobb
Bruce Durham

Ronnie Knight

Todd Ponder

2007

Don Black

Tony Farr

Mike O'Bryant

Linny Moore

Steve Cobb

Bruce Durham

Ronnie Knight

Todd Ponder

Curtis Steadman

Gregg Moore

Chris Walker

Rex Wilbanks

2008

Don Black

Steve Cobb

Bruce Durham

Tony Farr

Ronnie Knight

Gregg Moore

Linny Moore

Mike O'Bryant

Todd Ponder

Curtis Steadman

Chris Walker

Rex Wilbanks

2009

Steve Cobb

Bruce Durham

Kenny Hughes

Ronnie Knight

Albert McAbee

Gregg Moore

Todd Morris

Todd Ponder

Curtis Steadman

Earl Waldrop

Rex Wilbanks

Chris Walker

2010

Don Black

Steve Church

Kenny Hughes

Albert McAbee

Gregg Moore

Linny Moore

Todd Morris

Mike O'Bryant

Curtis Steadman

Earl Waldrop

Chris Walker

Rex Wilbanks

2011

Don Black
Steve Church
Bruce Durham
Tony Farr
Kenny Hughes
Albert McAbee
Linny Moore
Ronnie Knight
Todd Morris
Mike O'Bryant
Richard Vaughn
Earl Waldrop

2012

Don Black
Steve Church
Tony Farr
Bruce Durham
Larry Mason
Gregg Moore
Linny Moore
Ronnie Knight
Mike O'Bryant
Curtis Steadman
Richard Vaughn
Chris Walker

2013

Ben Dryden
Bruce Durham
Tony Farr
Kenny Hughes
Ronnie Knight
Larry Mason
Gregg Moore
Daniel Ross
Curtis Steadman
Richard Vaughn
Earl Waldrop
Chris Walker

2014

Steve Church
Ben Dryden
Kenny Hughes
Larry Mason
Gregg Moore
Linny Moore
Todd Morris
Mike O'Bryant
Daniel Ross
Curtis Steadman
Earl Waldrop
Chris Walker

2015

Steve Church
Steve Cobb
Bruce Durham
Ben Dryden
Tony Farr
Kenny Hughes
Linny Moore
Todd Morris
Mike O'Bryant
David O'Shields
Daniel Ross
Earl Waldrop

2016

Steve Church
Steve Cobb
Bruce Durham
Tony Farr
Ronnie Knight
Gregg Moore
Linny Moore
Todd Morris
Mike O'Bryant
David O'Shields
Curtis Steadman
Richard Vaughn

2017

Steve Cobb
Bruce Durham
Tony Farr
Trey Frick
Kenny Hughes
Ronnie Knight
Gregg Moore
David O'Shields
Chris Walker
Daniel Ross
Richard Vaughn
Earl Waldrop

2018

Steve Church
Trey Frick
Trent Henson
Kenny Hughes
Ronnie Knight
Gregg Moore
Linny Moore
Mike O'Bryant
Daniel Ross
Richard Vaughn
Earl Waldrop
Chris Walker

2019

Trey Frick

Daniel Ross

Kenny Hughes

Earl Waldrop

Linny Moore

Steve Church

Trent Henson

Mike O'Bryant

Bruce Durham

Tony Farr

Todd Morris

David O'Shields

APPENDIX IV
Called Out

In its 200-year history, Washington Baptist Church has produced generations of young people who have sensed the call of God upon their lives. Many have faithfully answered that call and have served the Lord around this world with great distinction. Here are the stories of some of these heroes. This list is in no way complete. The author realizes that there have been some who were probably overlooked, but this was in no way intentional.

SHANE BOWERS

Rev. Michael Shane Bowers was ordained by Washington Baptist Church in May 2012. His wife, Ashley, had been a lifelong member of Washington. Shane graduated from North Greenville University in 2007, and from Southeastern Baptist Theological Seminary with a Master of Divinity degree in 2011.

Shane and Ashley Bowers

Shane served as a North American Mission Board approved chaplain for seven years before resigning in 2019 to become a deputy coroner for Charleston County. He and Ashley make their home in Charleston. Ashley, who has earned her doctorate in education, teaches high school English in Summerville. They are both active in their local church.

CLYSTA HILL DE ARMAS

Clysta de Armas was saved at the age of seven in a revival meeting at Washington Baptist Church. It was at the tender age of thirteen that she really began sensing that God might use her in a much greater way.

Ralph and Clysta de Armas

Washington pastor O.B. Lancaster took Clysta under his wing and became a mentor who supported her in her ever-growing interest in missions. This desire in her heart was further fueled by her active participation in Washington's GAs.

It was while a student at North Greenville Junior College that Clysta made her definite commitment to a career in missions. After graduation from Furman, Clysta met and married Rafael (Ralph) de Armas, a native of Cuba. They enrolled in Golden Gate Baptist Theological Seminary, Mill Valley, California, and soon were employed by the Southern Baptist Home Mission Board and started a mission in Knightsen, California.

Castro's revolution in Cuba made it impossible for Clysta and Rafael to travel there after seminary graduation, so they settled in Florida and have spent most of their ministry working among Florida's large Hispanic population.

Clysta has served in many different capacities within the Southern Baptist Woman's Missionary Union. For four years, she was president of the Florida WMU, and was also elected vice president of the national WMU.

Clysta credits her love for missions to her early upbringing in the mission programs of Washington Baptist Church. She laments, "It is sad that many churches no longer have the children and youth organizations of WMU. That is where I received my training and my interest in missions." Thankfully, Washington made a commitment to retain these children's mission organizations. Because of this, there may very well be another Clysta de Armas waiting in the wings.

KERRY AND NELTIA HENDERSON

Kerry Henderson is a product of Washington Baptist Church. The son of Barbara and the late Joe Henderson, Kerry came through all the children's and youth programs of Washington and, as he grew into adulthood, became a leader in the church, serving in many different roles, including deacon.

Neltia was brought up in Apalache Baptist Church. The daughter of the late J.C. and Mary Lou Wilson, Neltia also had a strong and solid

Kerry and Neltia Henderson
Drayton, Isom, and McCain

Christian upbringing. She, too, learned much about missions through the mission education programs of her church.

After their marriage on May 23, 1992, Neltia joined Kerry at Washington and became actively involved in the life and ministry of the church.

It was during the interim ministry of Rev. Donel Kelley in 2000 that Kerry and Neltia first began hearing God's clear call to missions. A mission trip to Nicaragua galvanized these feelings. Thus, in the spring of 2001, the couple shared their decision with their church family and began to pursue their calling in earnest. Kerry soon enrolled at Southeastern Baptist Theological Seminary, and it was while attending there the Hendersons deployed to their first missionary assignment with the International Mission Board of the Southern Baptist Convention. This assignment took them to Tanzania, where they would work to evangelize the largely Muslim population and plant churches. It was during this time that Kerry received his seminary degree, and when they returned to the United States on furlough in 2005 they knew the Lord had closed the door to this opportunity in Tanzania.

It was in the fall of 2007 that Kerry and Neltia were first introduced to the "Every Village" organization, or, as it was known at the time, "Aid Sudan." In January 2008, they deployed once again to Africa — this time to Kampala, Uganda, where they worked to get the Gospel and physical aid into South Sudan. Their work flourished there until the spring of 2015, when they returned to the United States, only to learn that Neltia's father had recently been diagnosed with cancer. The family, which included sons Drayton, Isom and McCain, returned home to assist in the care of Neltia's dad and to ponder their future.

It was during this brief respite that the Hendersons were first introduced to Global Frontier Missions in Atlanta. Meanwhile, in October, 2015, Kerry was ordained to the Gospel ministry by Washington Baptist Church. In January 2016, the Henderson family once again moved — this time to Clarkston, Georgia, where they began their duties as pastoral care/member care directors for Global Frontier Missions. Not only were they busy working to reach the large and diverse population of immigrants in this area, they were also training and caring for the emotional and spiritual needs of future missionaries who were about to launch their careers on foreign mission fields.

Currently, Kerry serves as executive director for the Atlanta base of Global Frontier Missions. He also credits his strong commitment to missions to his early training through children's mission programs at Washington Baptist Church.

Larry and Denise Mason

LARRY MASON

Larry Mason is a Greer native and graduate of Greer High School. At the age of sixteen, he began sensing that God was calling him to the ministry, but his response to that call was delayed by several years. He graduated from both North Greenville Junior College and Limestone College. After a time in professional sales, Larry obtained a residential builder's license and developed the Mason Ridge subdivision, located just above Greer on Highway 290. Married to the former Denise Pritchett, Larry and Denise joined Washington in 2006 and immediately became actively involved in the church. In 2009, Larry was first introduced to the Men's Fraternity at Washington, and as a result of his deep involvement in this organization, he wrote a book entitled, *Casting Your Net: Eternal Things.* He said about the book, "The genesis of this book is born out of the question, how do I want to be remembered?"

It was during this time the Lord renewed His ministerial call to Larry, and Larry responded. On December 19, 2010, Larry made this decision publicly before the church and began to prepare to further pursue this call. Larry was licensed to preach by Washington Baptist Church on May 15, 2011. He was ordained as a deacon of the church in 2012, and continued his theological training at North Greenville University, where he received his Master of Christian Ministry degree in 2014.

Larry Mason was ordained to the Gospel ministry by Washington Baptist Church on July 5, 2015, having been selected to be the part-time pastor of Mountain View Missionary Baptist Church in Hendersonville, North Carolina, in May of 2015. He served there until June 2017. On July 1, 2017, he became pastor of Milford Baptist Church in Greer where he continues to faithfully serve at this writing. Larry and Denise are the parents of one daughter, Alexis, who is married to Tyler Norris. They have twin grandsons, Sawyer and Sutton.

KAREN PAESE

Karen Burnette Paese grew up in Greer and was a member of Washington Baptist Church from childhood. The daughter of the late Lee Burnette and the late Nell Mosteller Burnette, Karen was actively involved in Washington's GA and YWA programs under the leadership

Al and Karen Paese
Danielle and Julianna

of Mrs. Ruby Ross, Mrs. Joanne Barton and Mrs. Lettie Weeks. It was as a child and a teenager at Washington that she first began to sense that God was calling her to become a missionary. In the meantime, the Lord was issuing the same call to a young teenage boy in Pittsburgh, Pennsylvania, by the name of Al Paese. After meeting and marrying, Al and Karen began to pursue their lifelong dream of serving the Lord abroad. God designed a very specialized area of ministry for the Paeses. For twenty years, Al and Karen, along with their daughters Danielle and Julianna, served in Bandung, Indonesia, with the Network of International Christian schools from August 1996 until June 2016. Al taught middle school history, geography, and the Bible as well. Karen taught first grade for eight years and then served as the school librarian, along with teaching English as a second language.

Al had trained in sign language for the deaf before going to Indonesia, never dreaming that this skill would also open a great door for reaching a largely untouched people group. Al became one of the pastors and teachers of a deaf church in Bandung and also assisted an Indonesian pastor in beginning a deaf congregation in Sumatra, Indonesia. In 2004, the Paeses became affiliated with and supporters of the Bali Christian Orphanages in Bali, Indonesia. For the next sixteen years, they spent several weeks a year working with the children at the two orphanages. Al and Karen worked closely with their Muslim neighbors and friends, sharing the Gospel with them and teaching them to cook and develop other life skills. During this time, Washington Baptist Church was supporting the ministry of the Paeses through prayer and financial assistance.

After faithfully serving the Lord for all those years overseas, Al and Karen retired to Myrtle Beach. Al still works as an interpreter for the deaf in the public school system and is an interpreter in Ocean View Baptist Church, where they are members and where they still faithfully serve the Lord.

Joel and Amy Rainey
Sam and Seth

JOEL RAINEY

Joel Rainey is the son of Earl and Guynelle Rainey and was brought up in Washington Baptist Church from childhood. His parents were active members of the church, both serving in leadership capacities over the years. After high school graduation, Joel attended North Greenville University, where he received a Bachelor of Arts degree. He also earned the MDiv and PhD degrees from Southern Baptist Theological Seminary in Louisville, Kentucky. Joel was ordained to the Gospel ministry by Washington Baptist Church in 1998.

In 1994, he married the former Amy Lynn, and the couple have three children — Samuel, Seth and Grace. They currently live in Shepherdstown, West Virginia, where Joel serves as lead pastor of Covenant Church.

Joel has served as director of missions for the Mid-Maryland

Baptist Association as well as having been the state evangelism director for the Baptist Convention of Maryland/Delaware. He is currently an adjunct professor at both Anderson University and Southeastern Baptist Theological Seminary. He has also authored four books.

BIBLIOGRAPHY

Batson, Mann. *A History of the Upper Part of Greenville County, South Carolina.* Taylors: Faith Printing Company, 1993.

Batson, Mann. *Water Powered Gristmills and Owners.* Taylors: Faith Printing Company, 1996.

Batson, Mann. *A History of Reedy River Baptist Church.* Furman: Master's Thesis, 1958.

Flynn, Jean Martin. *History of the First Baptist Church of Taylors, South Carolina* Clinton: Jacobs Brothers, 1964.

Griffith, H.P. *The Life and Times of Rev. John G. Landrum (Reprint).* Columbia: South Carolina MAR, 1992.

Henerey, J.T. *History of Washington Baptist Church.* 1901.

Howard, James A. *Dark Corner Heritage.* 1980.

Kahl, Susan F. *The Bicentennial History of Brushy Creek Baptist Church Taylors, S.C., 1794-1994.* Brushy Creek Baptist Church, 1994.

Kinard, Joe Dew. *The Centennial History of the First Baptist Church of Greer, S.C., 1880-1980.* Columbia: R.L. Bryan Company, 1980.

King, Joe M. *A History of South Carolina Baptists.* Columbia: R.L. Bryan Company, 1964.

Lancaster, O.B. *How Washington Baptist Church Built Its Parsonage.* Smith Printing Company, Greer, South Carolina, 1946.

Langford, Vivian. *A Stroll Through the First 195 Years of Washington Baptist Church, Greer, S.C., 1819-2014.* 2014.

Langford, Vivian. *Pastors Washington Baptist Church, Greer, South Carolina 1819-2009,* 2009.

McCuen, Anne K. *Including a Pile of Rocks.* Greenville: Southern Historical Press, 2005.

Owens, Loulie Latimer. *Saints of Clay, The Shaping of South Carolina Baptists.* Columbia: R.L. Bryan Company, 1971.

Westmoreland, Lillie B. *J. Dean Crain, A Biography.* Greenville: Hiott Press, 1959.

Minutes of the Broad River Baptist Association, October 1820.

Minutes of the Tyger River Baptist Association, 1844.

Minutes of the North Greenville Baptist Association, 1911.

Minutes of the North Greenville Baptist Association, 1923.

Minutes of the Greer Baptist Association, 1959.

INDEX

C

E

F